The Kingdom, the Power, the Glory

The Kingdom, the Power, the Glory

Embracing the Mystery of the Lord's Prayer

Randal Earl Denny

Beacon Hill Press of Kansas City
Kansas City, Missouri

Copyright 1997
by Beacon Hill Press of Kansas City

ISBN 083-411-5964

Printed in the
United States of America

Library of Congress Cataloging-in-Publication Data

Denny, Randal Earl, 1937-
    The kingdom, the power, the glory : embracing the mystery of the Lord's prayer / Randal Earl Denny.
      p. c.m.
    Includes bibliographical references.
    ISBN 0-8341-1596-4 (hardback)
    1. Lord's prayer—Devotional literature.   I. Title
    BV230.D37   1997
    226.9'606—dc21

96-39976
CIP

10 9 8 7 6 5 4 3 2 1

To the people of Spokane Valley Church—
living holy lives,
letting people know Jesus,
loving one another—
a great example of the family of God.

Our Father which art in heaven,
Hallowed be thy name.
Thy kingdom come.
Thy will be done in earth, as it is in heaven.
Give us this day our daily bread.
And forgive us our debts, as we forgive our debtors.
And lead us not into temptation, but deliver us from evil:
For thine is the kingdom, and the power, and the glory,
for ever. Amen.

Matt. 6:9-13, KJV

Lord, Teach Us to Pray
Applying the Lord's Prayer to Life Situations
• • •

A Prayer to Lead Them
The Lord's Prayer Models Communication with God
• • •

A Lesson Plan for Prayer
The Master Teacher Offers the Key to Communication
• • •

Learning to Talk with God
The Lord's Prayer Maps the Way

CONTENTS

Preface

Let me tell you about a great inheritance I received from my father. During my elementary school years, World War II was being fought. My dad graduated from college as an older student, but jobs weren't very secure. One day he came home from work and told me he had lost his job. Then he said to me, "We'd better go upstairs and pray."

Up the stairs we climbed, and then we knelt beside the bed. Dad began to pray about his job situation—and our needs as a family. I turned to watch him and for the first time began to analyze what he was doing. Though I had said prayers before, at that moment I really began to understand that Dad was having a serious talk with God. It dawned on my young mind that God listens when we pray. But the best is yet to come.

While we were still kneeling beside the bed, we heard a knock on the front door. Mom called Dad. Someone was there to see him. I walked down a few steps to peek between the slats of the stairway banister. There stood a man I did not recognize, nor did Dad. With my own ears I heard him say, "I was just driving by your house and saw your old car. I wonder if you need a job."

Friends, that's not hearsay—it's firsthand. God answered dramatically that time so I could never explain it away. It is the single most important inheritance my dad gave to me. In my adolescent and youthful days I could never get away from the fact that God really does hear and answer prayer. Skeptics could never take that inheritance away from me.

The disciples who lived with Jesus noticed His habitual times of prayer. When near Him in prayer, they sensed the simple, almost childlike demeanor in His direct conversations with His Heavenly Father. Something about Jesus' vitality and frequency in prayer spurred the disciples to say, "Lord, teach us to pray" (Luke 11:1).

Jesus was quick to encourage His followers in prayer. He

simply said, "When you pray, say . . ." (v. 2). Then He began praying the most balanced, exemplary, simple yet profound prayer recorded in the Bible.

In this study of the popular Lord's Prayer, I want to share my spiritual pilgrimage in discovering the richness and the sacredness of this prayer so often uttered by mere rote.

I completed the journey of this book with a holy awe and profound respect for the Lord's Prayer. In my heart it stands almost as a sacrament for the community of believers as they recite it in unison. Yet in the privacy of my own thoughts and prayer time, the Lord's Prayer serves as a guide. As a rich treasury of truth, this model prayer somehow grows in importance as personal experience adds picture after picture to this album of prayer.

Will Durant once wrote about Oriental poetry with its rhyming of ideas rather than sounds of words. He said, "Chinese poetry combines suggestion with concentration, and aims to reveal, through the picture it draws, some deeper thing invisible. It does not discuss, it intimates; it leaves out more than it says. . . . 'The men of old,' say the Chinese, 'reckoned it the highest excellence in poetry that the meaning should be beyond the words, and that the reader should have to think it out for himself.'"[1]

That's what the Lord's Prayer is to us and so much more—words the reader has to think out for himself. Reading, meditating, and praying the Lord's Prayer will stimulate and encourage you to learn for yourself the deep meanings of Jesus' lessons on prayer.

Even as it has for me, I pray the Lord's Prayer will become holy ground for you too. Begin your adventure of learning to converse with God the Father.

Acknowledgments

Exposition, experience, and encouragement shaped me as I wrote this book. Quiet hours with God and His Book were augmented by persons who love the Lord's Prayer, and life experiences of answered prayer provided inspiration and ideas.

The experience of praying the Lord's Prayer with the people of God has shaped my spiritual life across many years. The excitement of preaching on the Lord's Prayer to my congregation at the Spokane Valley Church as well as to participants at the Nazarene Family Camp in British Columbia gave me the experience of sharing these lessons on prayer with people who are willing to respond to my inquiries about the subject.

The encouragement to put this material into book form came from many parishioners, my loyal staff, Dr. Charles Muxworthy of British Columbia, and especially my wife, Ruth.

I wish to acknowledge the following publishers for permission to quote material:

Charles Allen, *God's Psychiatry* (Fleming H. Revell Company).

William Barclay, *The Gospel of Matthew,* vol. 1 of the Daily Study Bible Series (Westminster Press).

J. B. Chapman, *Singing in the Shadows* (Kingshiway Press).

Paul Hetrick, "No 'Pay Back' at the Cross," *Herald of Holiness,* April 15, 1976.

W. Phillip Keller, *A Layman Looks at the Lord's Prayer* (Moody Press).

Walter Luthi, *The Lord's Prayer* (John Knox Press).

F. B. Meyer, *The Sermon on the Mount* (Baker Book House).

Willie B. Raborn, "A New Pair of Shoes," *Guideposts,* April 1976.

Haddon Robinson, "Prayer in the Life of Jesus," *Moody Founder's Week Conference Messages,* 1988.

John T. Seamands, *Tell It Well: Communicating the Gospel Across Cultures* (Beacon Hill Press of Kansas City).

Howard A. Snyder, *The Community of the King* (InterVarsity Press).

As in any time-consuming endeavor, I especially thank my wife, Ruth, for her encouragement to share what I have been learning about God and conversing with Him. She has always been a vital part of my ministry as well as my life. We have served as one, each doing what each one does best, as a divinely blessed team.

1

DISCIPLES WANTED TO UNDERSTAND PRAYER

Mystery: How can God be my Father?

Matthew 6:9-13; Luke 11:1-4

The disciples were curious about the power of prayers in the life of Jesus. Finally they asked Him to explain, and He did so by praying.

Dwight L. Moody, the Billy Graham of 100 years ago, understood the power of prayer when he said, "Every great movement of God can be traced to a kneeling Christian." Too often we forsake prayer for action. Some people practice prayer as a formal, routine ritual. Other people allow prayer to become flippant, disrespectful, irreverent. For many others, prayer isn't considered, discussed, or practiced until they are in some desperate crisis.

As Pastor John MacArthur Jr. explained, "Some people think prayer is like a parachute; they're glad it's there, but they hope they never have to use it."[1]

This crisis approach to prayer is illustrated in the story of a pilot who shouted over the radio: "Pilot to tower! Pilot to tower! I am 300 miles from land, 600 feet high, and running out of fuel. Please instruct. Over."

The distant voice responded: "Tower to pilot! Tower to pilot! Repeat after me: 'Our Father which art in heaven.'"

In Luke's Gospel, the reader is led several times to stand on tiptoe to watch Jesus kneeling in prayer. And the prayers of our Lord are much more than a parachute for tough times. Jesus' petitions are so lofty and the atmosphere so holy that we back out of the intrusion, not wanting to interrupt. Yet we are drawn again and again to hear Jesus praying, and we stand in awe at His source of power. Jesus takes all the mystery out of prayer by showing His disciples how to pray.

Jesus Planned for Prayer

Jesus' days were hectic and demanding like ours, but He did more than squeeze God into His schedule. He took time to pray. Even our Lord needed to pray, and He wanted to pray. On several occasions, Jesus spent an entire night praying. He kept close to God through that form of communication. Modeling this type of behavior no doubt heightened the interest of His disciples on many occasions and led one of the disciples to request, "Lord, teach us to pray" (Luke 11:1).

That request is one of the wisest prayers the Church or its leaders have ever uttered. My friend William McCumber suggested, "The mission of Jesus Christ is unsafe in the hands of a prayerless church. The devil fears nothing less than he fears a people who play at religion but do not pray."[2]

In response to their request, Jesus taught what is popularly known as the Lord's Prayer as an aid to conversation with God, not as a recitation. Rather than telling them how to pray, He prayed. And for nearly 2,000 years this prayer has taught Christian believers to pray.

FOR REGULAR CUSTOMERS

Listen closely to the opening request: "Lord, teach us to pray." The disciples addressed Jesus as "Lord." The Lordship of Jesus demands surrendered discipleship. That's a given. Jesus provided the Lord's Prayer to serious disciples committed to learning all He wanted them to know about himself and what He wanted them to become. No wonder many Bible scholars prefer to call it "the Disciples' Prayer."

The Prayer Was Once Reserved

The Early Church found believers referring to Jesus' prayer as the Prayer. In the first centuries of the Christian Church at Jerusalem, believers quoted the Prayer at the conclusion of Communion prayers, preceding the sharing of the bread and cup.

Public recitation of the Lord's Prayer was restricted to baptized church members. Part of the preparation for baptism required memorization of the Prayer.

Public recitation of the Lord's Prayer was restricted to baptized church members. Part of the preparation for baptism required memorization of the Prayer. Having identified with Jesus, believers prayed the Lord's Prayer three times daily as a reminder.

A scholar from an earlier generation, William E. Erb, noted, "The early Christians would not permit any person to use this prayer until he was baptized and made a profession of his faith. They regarded the sublime words of Jesus too sacred for the unconverted to repeat." He continues: "This prayer is in spirit not for those who are outside the church. . . . It belongs to those only who can offer it in humble and sincere faith."[3]

This reservation for serious disciples is the theme of a conversation that Southern Baptist Evangelist Roy Angell had with a woman who complained bitterly, "Why did God allow the hurricane to hit my house?"

"Are you a Christian?" Angell inquired.

"Well, no," she replied.

"Maybe God was busy taking care of His regular customers," the preacher said.

We Must Listen, Obey

If Jesus is Lord, disciples need to be open and available to Him. Living and working in a world filled with action and aggressiveness, we try hard to survive and to succeed. Yet moving into the world of prayer, we must adjust to being open and receptive to the Lord. We are accustomed to shoving and grabbing in the marketplace of our lives. In prayer, however, we must adjust our thoughts and actions to listening, to silence, to inactivity.

A mighty man of prayer, Robert Murray McCheyne, admitted that "a great part of my time is spent in getting my heart in tune for prayer." That's much different than the poetic phrase "Prayer moves the arm of God." Real prayer bows before the Lord as a servant waiting for "the arm of God to move

him." As we pray, we allow God to change us rather than trying to change the mind of God.

The first part of the Lord's Prayer relates to God's will and glory; the second part relates to man's needs.

This is why the first part of the Lord's Prayer relates to
God's will and glory, while the second part relates to man's
needs. Methodist missionary evangelist to India E. Stanley
Jones explained this relationship, "The first side [of the prayer]
is realignment and the second side is result. In the first side, we
realign life to our Father, to His name, to His Kingdom, to His
will; . . . in the second [part], we get the result—He gives us,
forgives us, leads us, delivers us." Jones underscores a profound prayer lesson: "The more you realign your purposes to
God's purposes, the more results you get. The emphasis, then,
should be on the realignment, and the result will take care of itself."[4]

The Lord's Prayer is designed for disciples who conscious-
ly seek to let God have His way and to yield themselves to His
will. That's the reason the prayer has only shallow significance
to nonbelievers.

Long ago I heard the story of a lawyer who was amazed
that his friend had begun teaching a Sunday School class. The
lawyer said, "I'll bet you don't even know the Lord's Prayer."

"Everybody knows the Lord's Prayer," his friend replied.
"'Now I lay me down to sleep.'"

"You win," the lawyer said with admiration. "I didn't
know you knew so much about the Bible."

A 30-SECOND SHORT COURSE

The disciples requested, "Lord, teach."

A striking feature of this instructional prayer is its brevity.
In Matthew's account in the King James Version, the Lord's
Prayer contains 66 words, 48 of which are one-syllable words. It
can be read aloud in less than 30 seconds. The prayer is simple,
yet profound; short, yet comprehensive. Following the prayer's
pattern, we learn the profound power of simple surrender.

God's greatest lessons often come in simple, unmistakable terms that everyone can understand.

The Lord's Prayer contains 66 words, 48 of which are one-syllable words. It can be read aloud in less than 30 seconds.

"Lord, teach." Learning to pray means more than saying a prayer. When they asked to be taught, what did the disciples have in mind? Jewish rabbis often taught congregations outline prayers known as "index prayers." The leader would recite a short sentence, followed by silence as the people meditated on that aspect of prayer. Each person would apply the truth to his or her own life. When Jesus' disciples asked, "Lord, teach," the Master Teacher outlined an index prayer.

Here's a profoundly simple lesson for all your praying. Pastor John MacArthur explains how: "If you concentrate on the Disciples' Prayer and work your way through its outline, no matter what you are praying about, you . . . have the confidence that you're praying the way Jesus taught."[5] As you saturate your prayers with the Lord's Prayer, you become immersed in the true disciples' way of life. Try it.

We Play Second Fiddle

By following Jesus' order in the prayer, you put God first and your requests second. Surprising but true, life eventually follows your prayers. Putting God first, we draw on His wisdom and put His will in the high priority it deserves.

As an early Christian leader who preached and wrote in about A.D. 200, Origen attributed a saying to Jesus that does not appear in the New Testament: "Ask the great things, and the little things shall be added to you. Ask the heavenly things, and the earthly things shall be added unto you."

It is appropriate to ask for bread to nurture life, bringing the needs of the present to the throne of God.

Origen notes that when you put God first and tune in to His will, you are then ready to ask for provision, pardon, and protection. It is appropriate to ask for bread to nurture life, bringing the needs of the present to the throne of God. Putting God first, however, makes Him a partner in ordering our lives.

Devotional writer William Barclay suggested that when we ask for bread to sustain our earthly lives, that request immediately directs our thoughts to God the Father, the Creator and Sustainer of all life. That's praying in the present tense. Learn to focus on God first, and you will tap in on His sufficiency for living. Jesus teaches us to "lay the present, the past and the future all before the footstool of the grace of God."[6] He is right. The Lord's Prayer brings the whole of our lives to God.

Barclay expanded the time dimensions of prayer when he said that asking for forgiveness directs our thoughts to God the Son, Jesus Christ our Savior and Redeemer. That's wonderful freedom from the past. When we ask for help to overcome future temptation, our thoughts are directed to God the Holy Spirit, Comforter, Strengthener, Illuminator, "Guide and Guardian of our way."[7] Putting God first, we find help for the present moment as well as the future and for the past. God's resources through prayer redemptively touch all three time dimensions: past, present, and future.

A Positive Spin on Life

The Lord's Prayer also teaches positive integration of life. Our request for bread leads to physical stamina, strength, and health. Our petition for forgiveness leads to mental well-being. Our request for help in temptation leads to spiritual stability. The Lord's Prayer directs us toward physical, mental, and spiritual wholeness. Every self-help section in bookstores everywhere demonstrates how hungry everyone in our culture is for such wholeness.

> **When you are puzzled over something you've prayed for, ask yourself: Can this request be covered by the petitions in the Lord's Prayer?**

When we ask, "Lord, teach," we begin to understand how a disciple of Jesus ought to pray. When you are puzzled over something you've prayed for, ask yourself: Can this request be covered by the petitions in the Lord's Prayer? If yes, you know you stand on solid ground for seeking God's help. Rest in the assurance.

A French student of the Bible said: "Let us read and re-read incessantly the Lord's Prayer. It is the true prayer of Christians and the most perfect, for it contains all."[8] What can anyone add to Jesus' prayer? Author and Pastor Aaron N. Meckel is right: "The Lord's Prayer is a blueprint, a chart and compass to guide us in our quest for God."[9]

I love the way the Lord's Prayer helps us build a habitual commitment to prayer. John Erskine, prolific writer and lecturer, said he learned the most valuable lesson of his life—a lesson we all need to learn about persistent, continuous prayer—when he was 14 years old.

His piano teacher asked, "How long do you practice?"

"An hour or more at a time," he replied.

"Don't do that," the teacher said. "When you grow up, time won't come in long stretches. Practice in minutes, whenever you can find them—5 or 10 before school, after lunch, between chores. Spread the practice throughout the day, and music will become a part of your life."

Erskine wrote most of his famous work, *Helen of Troy,* on streetcars while commuting between his home and the university.

Erskine said this advice enabled him to be a creative writer in addition to carrying out his duties as a professor. He wrote most of his famous work, *Helen of Troy,* on streetcars while commuting between his home and the university.[10] Consider applying this important lesson to your praying. In short moments throughout the day let the Lord's Prayer guide and shape your thoughts about God and life.

A GAME PLAN FOR THE TEAM

The disciples requested, "Lord, teach us."

No first person singular pronouns are found in the Lord's Prayer; rather, they are always plural. The word "us" is used four times. The pronoun "our" occurs four times; the prayer begins, "Our Father." The disciples said, "Lord, teach us." That's team learning—"us" and "ours."

"Pray for Each Other"

The plural pronouns show us that the Lord's Prayer is a team prayer. You learn football by playing as a team. You learn basketball as a team. Likewise, the basic way to learn to pray is with others and for others. When starting a prayer life, people sometimes make the common mistake of attempting alone to develop this relationship. The Bible urges, "Pray for each other" (James 5:16). You make quantum leaps at learning to pray by praying with others.

More than 500 million people today can say the Lord's Prayer from memory. That excitement and joy of walking through the prayer with millions is described by devotional writer F. B. Meyer:

> We cannot but think of the [millions] who have . . . been molded by the same sentences and thoughts and have found in these short but comprehensive petitions, expressions for their deepest, holiest moments.

Painting a word picture of this glorious awe, Meyer continues with a panoramic view of our fellowship in prayer:

> Lonely sufferers and crowded congregations, little children clasping their hands in prayer, and . . . saintly leaders of the Church, . . . Roman Catholic and . . . Protestant, . . . the servant and his master—all their differences of creed and station, sex or nationality, are forgotten as they enter together. . . . [The Lord's Prayer] is resonant with their voices, saturated with their tears, and ringing with their adorations.[11]

Just because the Lord's Prayer is a team prayer, each person who prays adds significance. Across two millennia, the whole Church from every corner of the earth becomes one in the prayer. The importance of every person in the prayer reminds me of the story about Leopold Stokowski taking over the mediocre Philadelphia Orchestra in 1912 and building it into one of the best—full of incredible sound, fire, and fury.

The orchestra's librarian had forgotten to distribute the fourth trombone part. The sensitive ear of the genius detected the missing notes.

Once, when rehearsing Stravinsky's *Rite of Spring,* he stopped the orchestra during a rousing passage. "I didn't hear the fourth trombone," Stokowski said. And he was correct. The orchestra's librarian had forgotten to distribute the fourth trombone part. The sensitive ear of the genius detected the missing notes.

Our Lord listens in the team prayer for your voice. He recognizes the distinctive tones colored by your praise, your petition, and your worship. You belong to His family and the community of faith. This communal act of prayer bearing His name has been kept sacred through the centuries. Its powerful meaning has been polished bright by the lips and voices of millions. The opening petition, "Our Father which art in heaven," makes us one.

Removing the How-to

As we study the Gospels, we see the disciples asking Jesus to teach them only one thing: "Teach us to pray." Jesus' prayer life influenced and impacted them. The more the disciples lived with Him, the more they knew they could not explain Him without understanding His praying. They realized His manner of praying was unlike what they had known. Eventually they had to ask, "Teach us to pray."

Earlier the disciples were sure they knew how to pray. After all, they knew the forms of prayer used regularly in their homes and synagogues. Doubtless since celebrating their own bar mitzvahs, they had all taken turns at leading public prayer.

As practicing Jews, they were praying men. Yet under Jesus' example they began to see the difference between saying prayers and really praying.

As practicing Jews, the disciples were men who prayed. Yet following Jesus' example, they began to see the difference between saying prayers and really praying. Such an admission represents the first step to spiritual growth. Paul said, "We do not know how we ought to pray" (Rom. 8:26, TEV). So the disciples enrolled in Jesus' short, intensive, life-changing school of prayer. And they were never the same again.

This modeling of prayer by Jesus for His disciples reminds me of a great story about Pachmann, the Russian pianist. In his 80th year he played a concert in London. Thousands of people listened breathlessly as he interpreted the works of Chopin.

At home afterward a woman asked her daughter, who was an accomplished musician, "Would you play something for us?"

Still under the spell of the master pianist, the daughter replied, "After Pachmann, who could play?"

The disciples felt that way about prayer after they had listened to Jesus praying.[12] Contemporary Christians sometimes feel the same way—who could ever pray like Jesus?

Satan delights in getting Christians bogged down in debates over how to pray. The Christian disciple needs to pray.

The disciples, however, did not get bogged down with techniques. They did not ask, "Teach us how to pray," but "Lord, teach us to pray." Satan delights in getting Christians bogged down in debates over how to pray. The Christian disciple needs to pray. Or as a popular advertising slogan says, "Just do it."

Jesus did not give a lesson on "how to pray." He responded to the disciples' request by praying, "Our Father which art in heaven" (Matt. 6:9, KJV). Technique is much less important than relationship and actually praying.

Pray by Just Doing It—Now

We cannot afford to get bogged down in method, technique, or strategy. We must begin now. As we acknowledge Jesus as Lord and follow His example, He enables us to communicate with God.

Guards caught a British soldier creeping into camp from the nearby woods. The charge was sharing secrets with the enemy, an incredibly serious offense. The soldier pleaded that he had gone into the woods to pray.

"Have you been in the habit of spending time in prayer?" the commanding officer growled.

"Yes, sir."

"Then get down on your knees and pray. You have never needed to pray as much as you do now."

The soldier, expecting death, knelt and poured out his heart in prayer with a spiritual authority that could have been inspired only by the Holy Spirit.

When the soldier finished praying, the officer said, "You may go. I believe your story. If you hadn't drilled often, you couldn't have done as well at review."

Get started praying. Use the Lord's Prayer to guide you. Like the soldier, drill often.

The power of praying the Lord's Prayer is illustrated in another story.

"Dad, I've got a great birthday present for you," Jeff told his father during a long-distance telephone call. "I quit smoking."

"How, Jeff?" his father asked.

"During my annual physical, the doctor said if I quit now, my lungs would suffer no permanent damage," said Jeff, a three-packs-a-day smoker. "I prayed the Lord's Prayer."

"You prayed the Lord's Prayer?"

"I knew it would be rough, so I made a vow to God that I would stop. I figured that I could let myself down, but I couldn't let God down. Every time I started to weaken and to reach for a cigarette, I'd say the Lord's Prayer. Sometimes I'd say it 40 times a day."

Jeff stopped smoking, his faith was strengthened, and his health was enhanced. He still says the Lord's Prayer every night—"just to thank Him."[13]

The Lord's Prayer, which can be recited in a short time, deserves lifelong practice. It not only will change your prayers but also will change your life.

A Conversation with God

Take the case of a hospital chaplain who stopped at a nurses' station and asked to see a woman whose door was closed.

"Don't go in there," the nurse warned. "She's unconscious. She won't know you're there."

"But I'm not going in just to see her," the pastor answered quietly. "I'm going in to speak to God about her."

Just as he expected, he found the patient unconscious, but he prayed and concluded by saying the Lord's Prayer aloud. To his surprise the patient suddenly joined in and whispered the closing words with him. The chaplain reported the incident to a nurse, and she shook her head.

"That woman's been in a coma for four days," she said.[14]

Prayer puts us in touch with God. What a privilege! What an opportunity! What an amazing relationship!

No wonder Jesus told His disciples "they should always pray and not give up" (Luke 18:1). It's God's good word to us too. Whatever your situation, the Lord's Prayer will enrich you and revolutionize you for the better. Never give up. Pray.

Chapter 1

Insights to Transform Your Praying

- Prayer is more than a parachute for tough times.

- Prayer challenges us to realign our will to the purposes of God.

- Prayer is simply profound.

- Prayer must be simply profound. The Lord's Prayer contains only 66 words, 48 of which are one-syllable words (Matthew, KJV).

- Prayer eventually shapes our lives.

- Prayer reaches across all time dimensions—past, present, future.

- One learns to pray by praying.

- God listens for every voice in the team prayers of His people.

2

ART, WHERE ARE YOU?

Mystery: Where does God live?

Matthew 6:9; Luke 11:2

"Art doesn't listen to me—it's no use," said the boy with a note of sadness. He had been praying for a bicycle.

Puzzled, his mother asked, "Art who?"

"Art in heaven," he replied.

Even adults with vague notions of Someone a long way up there in heaven have concluded that prayer is a wasted effort. To them the only available solutions seems to be more effort and better organization. They argue that prayer is a wasted motion and that prayer would not change God's purpose. Many give up on prayer because they have been disappointed so often.[1]

Poet Thomas Hardy had such deep problems with prayer that he came to believe that "prayer is useless because there was no one to pray to except 'that dreaming, dark, dumb thing that turns the handle of this idle show.'"[2] Put your ear down to his sentence and discover that even Hardy felt forced to believe that Someone turned the handle.

> **"We are all orphans. We would like to have a Father, but everything in the world seems to indicate that we do not have one."**

Viewing history as the story of humanity without a Father, German philosopher Goethe observed, "We are all orphans. We would like to have a Father, but everything in the world seems to indicate that we do not have one. . . . I shall be honest and not act as if I had a Father. Accordingly, I shall let prayer alone and rather talk to myself, like a child in the dark, a child who fears the dark, but will not admit it."[3]

For anyone who chooses to believe Goethe is right, there's a new "dial-a-prayer" for atheists. You call the number, but nobody answers.

Our greatest problem with prayer, however, is not atheism, but "a shadowy sense of God's reality"—to borrow Asbury Theological Seminary President Maxie Dunnam's phrase.[4] Jesus combats our out-of-focus image by teaching us to pray, "Our Father which art in heaven." Immediately He wants us to understand we are praying to a person, not to a cosmic process. We pray to a Father and not to a force. This simple address to a Father, signifying to whom we pray, turns out to be a profound description of God. Who can comprehend the reality that our God is also our Father?

WE PRAY TO AN INTIMATE GOD

Whether or not you comprehend this instruction, Jesus still said to pray, "Our Father."

Your concept of prayer depends on the kind of God you perceive. Jesus repeatedly referred to God as "Father." It's a revelatory, amazing idea. When Jesus was 12 years of age, He went to Jerusalem with His parents to celebrate the Feast of the Passover. As friends and family started home, Jesus stayed in Jerusalem without His parents' knowledge.

Much to their surprise and after three days of searching, Joseph and Mary found their Son and our Savior in the Temple courtyards, conversing with teachers. When Joseph and Mary scolded Jesus, He replied, "Didn't you know I had to be in my Father's house?" (Luke 2:49).

Jesus Modeled the Relationship

Jesus modeled intimacy with God the Father that was unknown among Jewish people. "They never considered themselves the children of God, but thought of themselves only as His servants," science and Bible teacher Harry Rimmer wrote in his book on prayer. "They believed in and feared Him, but never knew the joy of intimacy with Him."[5] Jesus changed all that forever.

The apostles, following Jesus' example, referred to God as "Father" 118 times in the record of their teaching and praying.

Jesus called God "Father" 226 times in the Gospels as He communed with His Heavenly Father. The apostles, following Jesus' example, referred to God as "Father" 118 times in the record of their teaching and praying.[6] Jesus showed them in the model prayer that praying was much like the relationship between a son and his dad.

In praying to God "our Father," we find He is not distant. He stays near to us. As the songwriter says, "He's as close as the mention of His name." Our Father God does not stand far away as though unconcerned. He draws close because He loves us. In that family closeness and friendly intimacy, we can just talk to Him.

The term "our Father" sometimes may be clouded by imperfections of earthly fathers. A study found that children's feelings about God usually reflect their relationships with parents, especially their father. Those with harsh parents are much more likely to fear God than those whose parents are loving. To those with loving earthly fathers, however, this title for God is exactly right, and for others it is a new joy to experience. "Our Father," the object of our prayer, is an intimate God who is loving, caring, and personally involved in our lives.

God's intimacy in that phrase, "our Father," assures us of four important facts.

We're All Family Members

"Our Father" includes us all. Because the word "our" amplifies "Father," this prayer belongs on the lips and in the hearts of every member of the family of God. God is Creator of all. But He is Father only to those people who have been adopted into His family. Creator and Father are not synonymous. God created everyone, but not everyone has been born into His family through Jesus Christ. But everyone can be.

A potter creates a work of art, giving full attention to the whirling clay being molded in his or her hands. After having finished with the vessel and having sold it to a customer, the potter is already busy shaping another vessel, not thinking much about the earlier product modeled by the same hands.

A real earthly father, unlike the potter, never loses interest in his children—whether he has 2 or 20. After all, each child bears something of his father's nature: a strong family resemblance in appearance and in character. Our Father cares about every child in His family. He creates us and redeems us. He sustains us, and we bear His likeness. He is better and nobler and more loving than all the earthly fathers of all of human history combined.

In Mark's Gospel Jesus refers to God as "Father" only when in the circle of His disciples.

In Mark's Gospel Jesus refers to God as "Father" only when in the circle of His disciples. Apparently the family concept was too annoying or threatening for nonbelievers to grasp. Yet in the Lord's Prayer all believers are invited to call God "our Father."

Do you remember the story about a police chief, Harold Bastrup, who had two copies of a photograph in which Ronald Reagan was standing between him and another police chief? Bastrup reasoned that it would make the picture more personal if he were to cut the other chief out of one photograph and to frame it. In a gesture of goodwill, he sent the second copy, uncut, to the other police chief.

There on the wall hung the photograph of the other chief standing alone with the president of the United States. Bastrup had been cut out of the picture.

Years later, Bastrup visited the other man's office. There on the wall hung the photograph of the other chief standing alone with the president of the United States. Bastrup had been cut out of the picture.

In the portrait of God's family no one is ever cut out.

In the family of God, we must invite others in when we pray. When we begin, "Our Father," we recognize our relationships with others. As Bible scholar Archibald Hunter enjoyed reminding his readers, "No man can be a Christian by himself. When we say The Prayer, we join ourselves with the whole family of God before the throne of grace."[7] To be a Christian is to be a member of God's family. We are all made kin and family by faith and grace.

An Open-door Policy

Our Father is continually accessible to us all. That means we can approach Him without fear, contrasted to a grown man who said, "My own father was emotionally uninvolved in my life and far away." Later that person reported his own feelings: "I projected this image of my earthly father onto God, my Heavenly Father. Consequently, I always felt that God was also far away and not too interested in my personal fulfillment and happiness."

A former professor of mine, Mendell Taylor, also a devotional writer, once said about calling God "our Father," "We are not confronted with a vast indifference or an aching void or an infinite blank. Instead, we behold the face of a heavenly Father who knows, who cares, who understands."[8] God awaits our conversation and responds with loving affection and encouraging affirmation.

Our relationship with God reminds me of the story of a Roman emperor, savoring his military triumph, who rode through the streets of Rome at the head of his marching troops. The roads were jammed with people cheering while Roman legionnaires struggled to hold back the pressing crowd.

A powerful soldier grabbed him and shouted, "You can't do that, boy. Don't you know who is in the chariot? That's the emperor."

A small boy burrowed through the spectators, darted between the legs of the legionnaires, and started toward the emperor. A powerful soldier grabbed him and shouted, "You can't do that, boy. Don't you know who is in the chariot? That's the emperor."

The boy laughed and said, "He's your emperor, but he's my father."[9]

You can imagine how quickly the boy was released to climb into his father's arms. Commenting on that story, author Robert Kopp wrote, "Every time we pray, 'Our Father,' . . . no one is lost in the crowd; . . . if we matter to no one else, we matter to God; . . . if no one else cares for us, God cares."[10] Think of the amazing reality—God our Father has a door open to you 24 hours every day across a lifetime.

He Knows My Name?

Our Father loves us all. The importance of this statement was heard in a little girl's prayer: "Our Father who art in heaven, how do You know my name?" Apparently she was not as impressed with a faraway God as with a God who knew her by name. Everyone, regardless of age, loves having a God who knows his or her name and loves each one of us.

The apostle John gave us two profound statements about the love of God: "God is love. . . . We love because he first loved us" (1 John 4:16, 19). We can lay aside foreboding fear or doubtful distrust because God loves us. The God of love welcomes us. He is always available to us and understands us even more than an earthly father understands his child's concerns.

> **For you did not receive a spirit that makes you a slave again to fear, but you received the Spirit of sonship. And by him we cry, "Abba, Father" (Rom. 8:15).**

The Bible teaches us about this blessed intimacy with God: "For you did not receive a spirit that makes you a slave again to fear, but you received the Spirit of sonship. And by him we cry, 'Abba, Father.' The Spirit himself testifies with our spirit that we are God's children" (Rom. 8:15-16). Paul fires up several relational ideas in quick, staccato fashion—sonship; *Abba*, Father; and God's children! Amazingly intimate!

A child whimpered as a worker of the Near East Relief organization made his way one night through an orphanage. The worker located the child and asked, "Are you sick, dear?"

"No," the child whispered.

"Do you have enough to eat?"

"Yes."

"Then what is the matter?" the man asked.

"I want somebody to love me," the girl replied.

For all who pray the Lord's Prayer, that Somebody is "Our Father."

In the Lord's Prayer, Jesus shows us that we are all loved. We have a Father. The more we recognize that fact, the more we exclaim, "How great is the love the Father has lavished on us, that we should be called children of God!" (1 John 3:1).

Gifts a Father Would Choose

Our Father provides for us all. The word Jesus used in the Lord's Prayer for "Father" means "Nourisher, Protector, Sustainer." That's the Father's role. Referring to provisions for our basic needs, Jesus said: "Your heavenly Father knows that you need them. But seek first his kingdom and his righteousness, and all these things will be given to you as well" (Matt. 6:32-33). Everything you need—really need—God will provide for you.

> **When I say the Lord's Prayer, I think of my earthly father—how good he was and how he loved to give me things.**

A parishioner's statement reminded me of this gift. She said, "When I say the Lord's Prayer, I think of my earthly father—how good he was and how he loved to give me things." That brings happy memories and wonderful hope to me too.

Ruth and I had been married three months. We were working at a YMCA camp, Ruth as a cook and I as the lifeguard. Our combined incomes were so small that we had only enough money to travel from California to Kansas City to attend seminary. The tires on our Volkswagen were bald. With our cross-country trip less than a week away, we had been doing some serious praying about tires.

One evening after supper, Mom and Dad drove up the dusty camp road. We were not expecting them. Dad rolled down a window and said, "Close your eyes."

Then Dad guided my hand to the backseat, where I felt

four new tires. To this day I don't know how my parents knew our need—they had never yet seen the Volkswagen we had purchased. But that image of Dad's delight in giving me a much-needed gift is as fresh and vivid as if it were this morning. He enjoyed giving us tires almost as much as we enjoyed receiving them.

It's a great prayer lesson too. Remember those incredibly significant words of Jesus: "If you, then, . . . know how to give good gifts to your children, how much more will your Father in heaven give good gifts to those who ask him!" (Matt. 7:11). What is true of my earthly dad is at least 10,000 times more true of our Father. He finds pleasure in making our lives meaningful. We pray to an intimate God who loves with an everlasting love as if each of us were the only one to love.

WE PRAY TO AN INFINITE GOD

Jesus instructed us to pray to our Father "in heaven." The Lord's Prayer is always to be prayed against that background of the heavenly world. Praying to an intimate God in heaven is almost too much to comprehend, too incredible to understand, and too amazing to accept. But let's look beneath, closer to the meaning of the prayer.

You're Talking to a Perfect Father

To overcome any imperfect image of fatherhood, Jesus added, "Our Father . . . in heaven." Psychologist and fellow pastor James Hamilton reminds us so powerfully, "God is like the best father you know if you subtract man's weakness from him and multiply the remaining good into infinity."[11] That's multiplication beyond my ability to imagine or think or grasp.

> **Whenever the Bible says that God is like a father, you can understand it means God is like a perfect father.**

Charlie Shedd imagines a child comparing the shortcomings and faults of his father with our perfect Heavenly Father. Such disparity can hinder a child's healthy understanding of God. Shedd suggested that dads tell their children, "Listen, troops. When I'm the kind of father I should be, that's what

God is like. Where I am not so hot, I hope you'll learn the all-important contrast.

"Whenever the Bible says that God is like a father, you can understand it means God is like a perfect father. You know I'm not perfect. But I'm going to keep on trying."[12]

Our intimate God is a perfect Father, better than all the most wonderful fathers in the world combined.

You're Not Talking to "the Man Upstairs"

The word "heaven" describes at least three different things in the Bible.

First, writers used "heaven" to refer to the earth's immediate atmosphere—the air and clouds where birds fly, wind blows, and rain falls.

Second, writers used "heavens" to talk about the expanse of space—the view of planets and stars, of sun and moon.

Third, biblical writers used "heaven" to portray God's realm, the New Jerusalem, the home prepared for His children, wherever He is.

God is as close as your faintest whisper.

Despite our songs, heaven is not some distant place "beyond the sunset." God is as close as your faintest whisper. Heaven describes the unspeakable difference between our world of sin and strife, of inequality and pain, of suffering and death, and God's realm of peace and truth, of love and grace, of eternity and holiness. Take heart, friends—God is in His heaven, and He leans close to hear your softest whisper to Him.

The Jewish phrase "which art in heaven" emphasizes the separateness of God. He is a holy God, unblemished by the stains of sin and evil so common in our world. God's holiness suggests He is above and apart from impurity. This state is described in the Old Testament passage "In the year that King Uzziah died, I [Isaiah] saw the Lord seated on a throne, high and exalted. . . . And they [seraphs] were calling to one another: 'Holy, holy, holy is the LORD Almighty; the whole earth is full of his glory'" (Isa. 6:1, 3). Imagine the love of our God, so full of splendor and glory, yet interested in the things that weigh heavy on our hearts. He stands apart from sin, but He moves in close to each one who calls His name. Our Father in heaven beckons even now, "Call to me and I will answer you and tell you great and unsearchable things you do not know" (Jer. 33:3).

From God's vantage point, He reaches down to us and lifts us to an uncommon level of life.

God Has a Long Reach

Best-selling author W. Phillip Keller clarified the idea: "The word heaven is derived from the old Anglo-Saxon word 'heave-on,' to be lifted up or uplifted. So it implies the thought of a place or a state which is above that of the commonplace condition on earth."[13] In other words, from God's vantage point, He reaches down to us and lifts us to an uncommon level of life. The Lord is quite prepared to raise us so that we can be with Him where He is.

Scientist Henry Norris Russell graduated from Princeton University with the highest honors in the school's history up to that time. As a scientist in the field of astronomy, he gave some inquiring young men head-splitting figures on the immensity of our universe. One fellow asked, "Dr. Russell, how is it possible that an infinite God can have time for us?"

A God who routinely cares for the universe and lovingly cares for me.

"The trouble is that your infinite God is not infinite enough," Russell replied. "If He is really infinite, He can dispatch the affairs of this universe in a twinkling of an eye and then have all the time in the world for you."[14] That's it—a God who routinely cares for the universe and lovingly cares for me.

One of the best fathers I know is my friend C. S. Cowles, who described a scene as his daughter, Deanna, attempted to ride her first bicycle.

"As she rode by," her father said, "I could see her front wheel begin to wobble. I was already halfway to her when she smashed up on our neighbor's lawn. No sooner had she hit the ground and let out that first blood-curdling scream than I was down beside her, gently untangling a hysterical girl from her twisted bike."

**With the application of medication
and the generous use of Band-Aids,
she was not only healed but soon
back out riding her bike again.**

After checking to make sure she had no broken bones, Cowles lifted his daughter in his arms, carried her into the house, and placed her on the kitchen counter.

"I dampened a clean cloth with warm water and carefully wiped the sand and dirt out of her scrapes and bruises," he said. "With the application of medication and the generous use of Band-Aids, she was not only healed but soon back out riding her bike again."[15]

That warm picture of a caring father reaching down and lifting up his child is a pale portrayal of our Heavenly Father, who reaches to us with infinite mercy and continuous compassion. He encourages us to make progress in life, but He stands ready to lift us up when we are wounded by life. He brings healing and wholeness, even after our failures and flops. Our Heavenly Father assures us, "Fear not, for I have redeemed you; I have summoned you by name; you are mine." As if that isn't enough, the passage continues, "When you pass through the waters, I will be with you; and when you pass through the rivers, they will not sweep over you" (Isa. 43:1-2).

God Owns It All

If God were small enough for our minds to grasp, He wouldn't be big enough for our needs. So Jesus shows us how big God is when He teaches us to pray, "Our Father . . . in heaven."

Professor Lyle Pointer tells about a boy who asked his father's help in repairing a wagon. When the job was done, the boy looked up and said, "Daddy, when I try to do things by myself, they go wrong. But when you and I work together, they turn out just fine."[16]

God is like that in His care for us. Our Heavenly Father reminds us, "'For I am the LORD, your God, who takes hold of your right hand and says to you, Do not fear; I will help you. . . . For I myself will help you,' declares the LORD, your Redeemer" (Isa. 41:13-14). I'm glad we can belong to Him!

Jesus wants us to draw on the infinite resources of our intimate Heavenly Father. We pray to a loving, intimate God who is also infinite and holy.

WE PRAY TO AN ETERNAL GOD

Jesus said to pray, "Our Father which art." Two profound lessons lie under the surface in the verb "to be."

God Never Plays Hooky

First, our Father God is here for us now. What an assertion and what an affirmation! "Our Father which art." Aaron Meckel rightly reminds us that Jesus never argued the existence of God. He assumed it and brings us to God.[17] Scripture says, "In the beginning God" (Gen. 1:1) and "The Lord is" (Ps. 23:1). In other words, God always was even as He now is. People tend to forget that fact or never grasp it.

A Christian teacher was spending his summer vacation on the coast of Maine. On an island offshore, he found a group of children who had no Christian training. He made arrangements to visit their island and to teach them on Sunday mornings.

He used the technique of starting with something close at hand and familiar to the children. He asked, "If you have seen the Atlantic Ocean, raise your hand."

Not a hand went up. Thinking the children must be timid, the teacher asked the question again. It turned out that the children were quite sure they had never seen the Atlantic Ocean, even though they had been surrounded by it, had played beside it, and had sailed their boats near its shore. Yet they did not realize it was the Atlantic.

God is like that. He is ever present with us, even when we fail to recognize Him.[18]

God is here for us each moment of our day. The Bible assures us, "Seek the LORD while he may be found; call on him while he is near" (Isa. 55:6). Helen Steiner wrote, "No one ever sought the Father and found He was not there." I rejoice in the fact of God's presence with me day after day.

In a train compartment, a Muslim passenger got out his prayer rug, knelt, and went through his prayer ritual. John T. Seamands, a Methodist missionary to India, asked him, "Can you please share with us what prayer means to you?"

"Honestly, all this praying doesn't mean much to me," the Muslim said without hesitation. "It is just a routine that I do out of a sense of duty."

Admitting that at one time in his life prayer was a dry ritual, Seamands testified, "I, too, prayed as a matter of duty. But then I came to know [Christ] as my personal Savior and Lord, and since then prayer has taken on new meaning. It is like a son talking to his father. When I pray, I feel His presence very near."[19]

I'm glad we can move beyond mere rote words and enjoy intimacy with a personal God who loves us dearly.

> **Our Heavenly Father never tires of hearing His children call to Him. He never deserts them. He awaits their prayers.**

Someone You Can Depend On

Nearly 2,000 years ago Jesus taught His people to pray, "Our Father which art." If this world holds together for 2,000 more years, God's people will still be saying, "Our Father which art." Our Heavenly Father never tires of hearing His children call to Him. He never deserts them. He awaits their prayers.

The Bible explains, "Without faith it is impossible to please God, because anyone who comes to him must believe that he exists" (Heb. 11:6). People will never be able to say accurately and honestly, "God was."

Let me explain. Earl W. Denny was my father. But I can pray to One in heaven, "You are my Father." And during all of eternity, He is my Father. "'I am the Alpha and the Omega,' says the Lord God, 'who is, and who was, and who is to come, the Almighty'" (Rev. 1:8). Since He's here with us for the long run, it's a good idea to keep in touch with Him.

Listen once again to the important first 6 words in the Lord's Prayer: "Our Father which art in heaven." The remaining 60 words explain these words and apply them. These 6 words are the confession of a child of God. The remainder of the prayer is actually wasted until you make the decision: "I will arise and go to my [F]ather" (Luke 15:18, KJV). Novelist H. G. Wells once said, "Until a man has found God, he begins at no beginning and works to no end." God alone gives meaning to the whole of life.

During a long war, a father was separated from his family. When he returned, his children no longer recognized him. Everyone felt awkward. The mother even had to tell the children to shake hands with their father. Is the Father, who is in heaven, a stranger to you? Do you feel awkward in His presence? Do you know Him anymore?

Pastor Charles L. Allen, long-term and well-loved pastor of First Methodist Church in Houston, told the story of a girl whose mother had died and whose father had disappeared and was presumed dead. The girl had no memory of love, and she suffered the pangs of loneliness.

Her father was alive, however, and was a successful businessman. His search for his daughter led him to a cheap boardinghouse in Atlanta. There he knocked on a door, introduced himself to his daughter, and said, "I have come to take you home."

After confirming his identity, the young woman moved out of the boardinghouse to live in a beautiful home with her newfound father. "No one can ever know what it means to me when I discovered that I had a father," she said.[20]

Have you made that discovery about God? Is He your Father—yet? Jesus prayed, "Father, the time has come. . . . Now this is eternal life: that they may know you, the only true God, and Jesus Christ, whom you have sent" (John 17:1, 3). How good to know that you have a Heavenly Father, eagerly waiting for you to come home!

Chapter 2
Insights to Transform Your Praying

- Prayer is directed to a loving Father, not to a cosmic process or force.

- Jesus used the loving word "Father" 226 times in the New Testament.

- No one can be an effective Christian alone.

- Our Father God is always accessible.

- God responds to our prayers with attention and affirmation.

- What is true of an earthly dad is at least 10,000 times more true of our Heavenly Father.

- With God no one is lost in the crowd.

- Everything you really need God has on reserve for you.

3

WHAT AN ADORABLE NAME!

*Mystery: Why would a holy God
be interested in me?*

Matthew 6:9; Luke 11:2

If we tried to compose a prayer in the spirit of our times, we would probably begin with ourselves and our needs. Jesus, however, taught His disciples to focus their prayer on God: "Our Father which art in heaven, Hallowed be thy name" (Matt. 6:9, KJV). Where prayer is first focused makes all the difference.

A boy in Connecticut innocently prayed, "Our Father which art in New Haven, Howard is Thy name." We may understand his confusion, because nothing seems sacred or holy or hallowed anymore. Most of us learned the Lord's Prayer by rote from the revered language of the King James Version of the Bible. But this first petition of the Lord's Prayer probably is the least understood. The four words "Hallowed be thy name" paint a strong picture of adoration for God the Father.

One of my seminary professors told of three sisters who sang "The Lord's Prayer." The children had trouble pronouncing the word "hallowed."

"When they sang the prayer it sounded more like, 'How loaded is Thy name.' Maybe they really had something. God's name is loaded with grace and power and glory with abounding benefits and overflowing blessings."[1] What is the key to learning the lesson of this prayerful petition—"Hallowed be thy name"?

Devoted to Sacred Purposes

The word "hallowed" means "to be devoted to sacred purposes." It carries the idea of holiness, sanctity, reverence, and worship. "Hallowed" comes from the Greek noun for "holy." Jesus' petition suggests "to keep holy" or "to sanctify in our hearts." It is defined in a word study as "Let Your name be sanctified."[2]

Our English word "holy" comes from Anglo-Saxon words, "halig" and "hale," which describe something or someone set apart, unique, healthy, or whole. Popular writer W. Phillip Keller clarifies further: "People say, 'Oh, I'm hale and hearty,' meaning that the person is in excellent health, wholesome and fit."[3] God is all that and so much more. Our Father in heaven is totally complete, more than adequate, loving and nearby, so we revere Him.

> **Our Father in heaven is holy—
> completely free from impurity,
> incompleteness, and selfishness.**

To help us understand more completely the implications of the holiness of God, Peter quoted from the ancient Scriptures: "Just as he who called you is holy, so be holy in all you do; for it is written: 'Be holy, because I am holy'" (1 Pet. 1:15-16). Our Father in heaven is holy—completely free from impurity, incompleteness, and selfishness. And He wants us to be holy.

The hallowedness of God caused the old Jewish prayer called a kaddish to include, "May His great name be magnified and hallowed in the world." Critics of Jesus attack His originality because He apparently used such parallels to form this part of the Lord's Prayer. That should not shock us, Archibald Hunter reasons, because "the work of a great artist is not to manufacture his paints, but with them to paint a beautiful picture. So Jesus, using older materials, made His perfect prayer."[4] Whether ancient or modern, we begin prayer by revering, worshiping, and adoring a holy God, not just a friendly old chum.

**A coin's image becomes worn and blurred
as it passes through many hands. God's
name can also be worn down
by careless usage even among
religious people.**

Our lips form the familiar petition, "Hallowed be thy name." What is its value to us? A coin's image becomes worn and blurred as it passes through many hands. God's name can also be worn down by careless usage even among religious people. Jesus intended for the first petition of His prayer to keep the Fatherhood of God and His holy nature clear in our minds.

A Point of Purification

In Jerusalem I once watched Muslims wash their feet before entering their mosque to pray. They wanted to be absolutely sure of being clean when they prayed. Jesus places the sentence "Hallowed be thy name" at the beginning of the Lord's Prayer to help us wash our hearts and minds and mouths as we enter the sanctuary of prayer with "Our Father."

As devotional writer Edward Vick shows the way "hallowed" connects to earlier parts of the prayer, "There is a definite relationship between the first two clauses of the Lord's Prayer. The God to whom we speak and to whom we listen invites us to come to Him as His children. But any danger of our familiarity with Him is immediately corrected by the clause 'Hallowed be thy name.' We cannot speak of God in just any way we wish simply because He is our Father. He is also holy."[5] While Jesus invites us to talk to God as our Father, He also insists on respectful reverence for our holy God.

The first petition in this prayer has at least three meanings:

REVEAL YOURSELF TO US

In our quest for understanding of God and His ways, we pray, "Hallowed be thy name." In biblical times the name stood for the nature of a person. To know God's name would be to understand His nature. By His name He reveals himself to us. "Hallowed be thy name," therefore, means "reveal yourself to us."

Names often identify qualities of character. In his book *A Layman Looks at the Lord's Prayer*, W. Phillip Keller notes that he feels a bit more confident about his safety while flying when he sees the twin-Rs insignia on the jet engines, signifying they are made by Rolls Royce. For him the name represents the most advanced research and bears the stamp of meticulous care and precision that "symbolizes reliability and dependability, craftsmanship and design."[6] Such awareness helps offset the fact that the airplane itself was built by the lowest bidder.

We can rest on the dependable and meticulous reliability of our Heavenly Father. "Hallowed be thy name" causes us to find assurance and expect dependability from God as He reveals himself to us.

I AM WHO I AM

God's name reveals His trustworthiness and His eternal faithfulness. During the burning bush experience in the deserts of Horeb, for example, God called Moses to deliver His people out of Egyptian slavery.

You remember the incident. "Moses said to God, 'Suppose I go to the Israelites and say to them, "The God of your fathers has sent me to you," and they ask me, "What is his name?" Then what shall I tell them?'

"God said to Moses, 'I AM WHO I AM. This is what you are to say to the Israelites: "I AM has sent me to you"'" (Exod. 3:13-14).

> **You shall not misuse the name of the LORD your God, for the LORD will not hold anyone guiltless who misuses his name**
> **(Exod. 20:7).**

The Hebrew word for the name God gave himself has four consonants. It is the word "Yahweh," which means "I AM" or "I AM WHO I AM." Later, while delivering the Ten Commandments, God declared, "You shall not misuse the name of the LORD your God, for the LORD will not hold anyone guiltless who misuses his name" (Exod. 20:7). We must learn and express a serious reverence for God's name.

In an effort to revere that name, Jews would not pronounce the name "Yahweh." When they came to that word while reading their scrolls, they would pause in silence before continuing. Eventually they substituted the name "Adonai," which means "Lord." With the passage of time, Jewish writers took the consonants of Yahweh and added the vowels of Adonai to create the word "Jehovah." This artificiality resulted from their effort to hallow God's name.

Jesus encouraged us to pray, "Hallowed be thy name," or "Let Your name be revealed to us." It is our sincere quest to know God and to understand what He reveals about himself. On the eve of His crucifixion, Jesus prayed for His disciples, "Righteous Father . . . I have made you known to them, and will continue to make you known" (John 17:25-26). In response to our request to hallow God's name, the Lord seeks to reveal His true nature to us.

A Name You Can Count On

The dependability of God gives us confidence continually, even in the storms of life. Near Cologne, Germany, anguished men hidden in a bunker during World War II wrote on the walls, "I believe in the sun even when it is not shining. I believe in God even when He is silent. I believe in love even when I feel it not." You can count on God when you hallow His name in your prayers.

Long ago the psalmist sang, "Those who know your name will trust in you, for you, LORD, have never forsaken those who seek you" (9:10). In my own experience I can testify to the dependability of God. And so can you.

God, the One whose name we hallow and adore, is not like the Asian prince who wished to teach his son about the cruelties of life. Placing the boy on a high ledge, the father coaxed him to jump into his arms. The boy was encouraged to repeat jumping until all fear was gone. Then, on the last jump, the father stepped away, and his child fell to the ground. The father told his whimpering son, "Let this be a lesson to you. Never trust anyone, not even your own father."

What a contrast with our Father, who will never let you down! He never fails His children. Over and over God says, "I will never leave you nor forsake you" (Josh. 1:5). Scripture promises, "The eternal God is your refuge, and underneath are the everlasting arms" (Deut. 33:27). That's good news. We have a God who never leaves us, who serves as our Refuge, and who supports us with His everlasting arms. That sounds like sufficient support for every situation, and it is.

While the word "holy" rings out as one of the main words of the Old Testament, the key word in the New Testament is the word "Father."

We can confidently pray, "Let Your name be revealed to us." To whom are we speaking? What name? The One to whom Jesus taught us to pray, "Our Father which art in heaven." While the word "holy" rings out as one of the main words of the Old Testament, the key word in the New Testament is the word "Father." Supreme Court Justice Oliver Wendell Holmes Jr. said his faith could be summarized in the two words "our Father." In his discussion concerning prayer, William Erb brought this issue into clear focus. "The name by which we address God indicates our conception of God."[7] To what kind of God do you pray? It must be the Holy Father.

A Salvation Army worker urged a woman in the slums of a great North American city to simply talk to God as a friend.

"Dear Sir, I am sorry to trouble You, but . . . ," the woman began. Then words of her misery flowed from her heart. She concluded her prayer, "Yours sincerely," and added her name.

As she learns more of God as "our Father," the more she will understand the goodness and grace of His character, and the more her intimacy with the Lord will increase. Our eternal Father is here with us. Never austere and uncaring, He is never the One from whom we must wring each little blessing. He loves us and provides for us. He loves us willingly and always has our best interest in mind.

BE RELEVANT FOR US

When we pray, "Hallowed be thy name," we must become aware of the necessity of submission to God. With the passage of centuries, the Lord's Prayer became a mantra—a prayer chanted so fast and so repetitively that it lost meaning. Perhaps we all have done that sometime when praying this prayer.

Author Leslie Flynn suggests the prayer was repeated so rapidly during medieval times that its opening word in Latin gave rise to the English word "patter," an abbreviation of "paternoster," which means "Our Father."[8] Checking *Webster's New Collegiate Dictionary*, I discovered that "patter" was defined as empty chattering talk, a quick succession of slight sounds, to say or speak in a mechanical or rapid manner, to recite prayers rapidly or mechanically.

"Hallowed" helps us resist the temptation of routine praying. Jesus wants us to bring our wills into loving compliance to His purposes for us. Such submission begins the process of setting our wills to do the will of God. I want to learn His will and do it, not try to convince Him to do my will. Submission is an important key to a happy, holy relationship with God.

A Sense of Unworthiness

A submissive spirit starts with an awareness of our unworthiness. When we pray, "Our Father," we realize how little we have hallowed and adored His name. We know we can do nothing to make God love us more, but we can rejoice in the fact that we can do nothing to make Him love us less.

> **God never allows us to live one way and pray another. God's name must become relevant to our living and to our attitudes.**

Let's admit it—we have not always behaved in ways that hallow God's name. Our relationships with others reflect the degree with which we hallow His name. Relationships are often God's examination time. He never allows us to live one way and to pray another. His name must become relevant to our living and to our attitudes.

If God is holy, then we never honor God's name by unholy thoughts or behavior. The Bible says, "Everyone who confesses the name of the Lord must turn away from wickedness" (2 Tim. 2:19). Each of us must pray, "Let Your name be sanctified in me today." Such a prayer pushes us to live in acceptable, Christ-honoring ways.

Full Surrender Required

A submissive spirit produces full surrender. Knowing God intimately gives us confidence to surrender our lives to Him. We honor the Lord by giving Him the throne of our hearts, so He becomes Lord of all in us. The Bible challenges, "In your hearts set apart Christ as Lord" (1 Pet. 3:15). It's a satisfying way to live.

There is a vivid illustration of this full surrender in the story of a minister who was jealous of D. L. Moody's success as an evangelist. The envious clergyman, in a committee convened to call an evangelist for a citywide crusade, was disturbed by everyone's eagerness to invite Moody as the speaker.

The disgruntled pastor asked, "Does Moody have a monopoly on the Holy Spirit?"

"No," was the reply, "but the Holy Spirit has a monopoly on Dwight L. Moody."

That's the secret of full surrender. God not only used Moody but also will use anyone whose life reflects a submissive attitude to the Lord.

Grow Through Obedience

A submissive spirit grows in obedience. Consistent obedience to God's Word continually hallows and honors His name. Jesus urged, "Let your light shine before men, that they may see your good deeds and praise your Father in heaven" (Matt. 5:16). We cannot hallow God's name apart from doing His will. Martin Luther once asked: "How is God's name hallowed amongst us?" Then he answered his own question: "When both our doctrines and our living are truly Christian."[9] The same answer works in every age. Either we hallow His name with obedience, or we desecrate His name with disobedience.

"Hallowed be thy name" means we put God in charge of our life. I know a Christian businessman in Modesto, California, named Bud LaCore. He owned a tire business. An employee struggled with submitting to authority, resisted supervision, and refused to follow Bud's instructions.

One day Bud took the fellow by the arm, led him to the street, and turned him around so that he could see the sign over the store.

"What does that sign up there say?" Bud asked.

"It says, 'LaCore Tire Company,'" the employee replied.

"I am LaCore," Bud said firmly.[10]

Submission means we give ourselves totally to God because He already owns everything we hold so tightly in our hands.

The lesson on submission means we really pray, "Let Your name be relevant in us. Let us be submissive to Your name and to Your leadership in our lives."

A NAME TO BE REVERED

Awareness plus submission equals reverence. Moffatt translated his first petition, "Thy name be revered." We revere God by giving Him first place in our hearts and first place in our priorities. Another Bible authority paraphrased the idea of giving God reverence like this: "Enable us to give [You] the unique place which [Your] nature and character deserve and demand."[11] Yes, God is worthy of our praise. Genuine prayer builds on reverence. You can't worship Him if you don't respect Him.

Focus on Our Father

We revere God by concentrating on our Father. It's so much easier to shut the door of our room than to shut the door on thoughts that crowd our minds when we begin to pray. I'm sure we have all struggled with the problem, though it is not a new one.

Long ago preacher John Donne described a common experience: "I throw myself down in my chamber, and I call in, and invite God and His angels thither. And when they are there, I neglect God and His angels for the noise of a fly, for the rattling of a coach, for the slamming of a door." It's easy to be distracted during prayer.

Thinking of this common experience, scientist Harry Rimmer reminded us that prayers are hindered when we forget that we are talking to "the Father Almighty, Maker of heaven and earth." But, Rimmer continues, nothing could "strain the capacity of our faith" when we grasp the greatness of God. If we consider the holiness of God, "We would not ask for any unworthy thing."[12] Do you remember into whose presence you have come when you pray?

Jesus lived out the prayer by revering God in thought, in speech, in deed, and in worship.

We should revere God by our living. We honor His name with our lips, our thoughts, our lives, our families, and our vocations. Jesus once prayed, "Father, glorify your name!" (John 12:28), and then lived out the prayer by revering God in thought, in speech, in deed, and in worship. Reverence cannot be turned on and off like a faucet of water; it must permeate all parts of our lives.

We should revere God in our use of spiritual resources. This means our hunger and respect for Scripture will grow. It means we would honor the Lord's day, which is increasingly being ignored by people in pursuit of pleasure. It means that we would revere the holy sacraments as we observe them with joy and thanks. It also means we revere God's people and spiritual leaders. Reverence shows we are serious about our relationship to God.

We should revere God continuously. One of my favorite commentators once observed, "To reverence God means to live in a God-filled world, to live a life in which we never forget God. This awareness is not confined to the church or to so-called holy places; it must be an awareness which exists everywhere and at all times."[13] I love that idea of living in a God-filled world—office, home, school. Does your reverence for God affect what you do and where you go?

The classified advertising section of the *Tribune* newspaper in Kokomo, Indiana, carried personal messages like birthday greetings, Valentine notes, and love letters.

"Thank you, Shirley Slusser, for 18 years of wedded bliss," one item read. "You are the most wonderful, beautiful wife in the world, and I love you more than ever. If it were not for the fact that I promised Dan, Larry, and George that I'd play pool tonight, I'd certainly be with you on the anniversary of the most important day of my life."

I love You, Lord. I'm committed to You. Being Your child is a high privilege, but today, once again, I'm ignoring You, neglecting our meeting. I have too many other things on my agenda.

That message sounds familiar. "I love You, Lord. I'm committed to You. Being Your child is a high privilege, but today, once again, I'm ignoring You, neglecting our meeting. I have too many other things on my agenda. Sorry about that."

We need to hear it again. We need to pray it again: "Hallowed be thy name," or "Let Your name be revered in us." To pray that phrase with meaning, we must know who God is and submit ourselves entirely to His Lordship.

Maxie Dunnam underscores the need for revering God: "One of the glaring limitations of many modern expressions of the Christian faith is that God is domesticated, reduced to a good friend next door—or upstairs—who is always there to attend to not only our needs but our wants."[14] The psalmist called something much higher to our attention: "Glorify the LORD with me; let us exalt his name together" (34:3). That should be the spirit of our reverence of God.

A Name That Leads the List

In this discussion of the Lord's Prayer, "Our Father" has been placed at the beginning to emphasize that God is our Source for being wholly His. Scripture affirms what we already know: "Every good and perfect gift is from above, coming down from the Father" (James 1:17).

I have heard that Christians in some places in the West Indies sing a unique rendition of the Lord's Prayer. After each petition, the phrase "Hallowed be thy name" is sung as a chorus. That repetition rivets each thought of the Lord's Prayer to the holy name of God. What a delightful practice! That phrase should be joined to every human experience.

Willie Learns a Lesson

Willie Raborn was a teenager in 1963. Keeping up with the "in" crowd seemed important. If you didn't wear the faddish penny loafers, you might as well go barefoot, he said.

Because Willie had new oxfords, he surprised his father by asking for money for another pair of shoes.

"Willie, the shoes you have on aren't a month old yet," his father said. "Why do you need new ones?"

"Everybody's wearing penny loafers, Dad."

Raborn, whose income as a mechanic barely covered rent and groceries, discussed the matter with Willie and then said, "Son, wear those shoes one more day. Look at every pair of shoes you see at school. If you can come here after school and tell me that you're worse off than the other kids, I'll take part of your mom's grocery money for you to buy some new shoes."

The next morning, Willie noticed all the different kinds of shoes, but he was determined to have penny loafers with horseshoe taps on the heels.

All he could see were his father's legs sticking out from under a car. As he waited, he noticed that his father's shoes were old.

After school, Willie went to his father's shop. All he could see were his father's legs sticking out from under a car. As he waited, he noticed that his father's shoes were old. The left shoe had two stitches of baling wire where the soles had separated. The laces on both shoes had been spliced. Neither shoe had a heel, only small, bent nails where heels had been.

At last, his father scooted out from under the car and gave Willie money for the shoes and sales tax. Willie ran two blocks and stopped in front of the shoe store window. There he gazed at the shoes.

As Willie stood there, he couldn't help but remember his father's shoes, the mended soles, the spliced laces, the bent nails, the baling wire. Willie wondered whether his father's feet got cold on wintry nights helping people start their cars. But he couldn't recall his father ever complaining.

The gleam on the penny loafers began to dull in Willie's mind as he went inside the store and stopped near a rack of shoes bearing the sign Clearance—50% Off. Below the sign he saw new versions of his father's work shoes.

"My mind was playing Ping-Pong," Willie said later. "First, Dad's old shoes and then the new ones. First the image of me keeping up with the 'in' crowd at school, and then this image of Dad—tireless, selfless, almost Christlike in the sacrifices he was willing to make for his family. When it came to 'keeping up,' which ideal was worth following?"

Willie took a size 10 from the clearance rack and raced to the checkout counter.

"I ran back to the shop and put Dad's new shoes in his car," Willie said. "Dad picked up the box when he got in the car. When he opened it, he just stared without saying a word. He looked first at the shoes and then at me."

"I thought you were going to get those penny loafers," Willie's father said.

How could he tell his father that he had chosen to mirror his image?

"I was, Dad, but . . ." Willie couldn't explain the rest. How could he tell his father that he had chosen to mirror his image? Or that when it came to "keeping up," Willie had decided to try to keep up with the very best?

"I wanted to be more like the good man God had given me for a father," Willie said.[15]

What Willie said about his earthly father is similar to what we should say to our Heavenly Father. That's what we mean when we pray, "Hallowed be Thy name, an image I have chosen to follow." We want to be more like the Father whose name we honor.

Chapter 3

Insights to Transform Your Praying

- We pray to a holy God, not to a friendly old chum.

- You can count on God even in the storms of life.

- Our Lord wants us to bring our will into loving compliance to His will.

- Submission is the key to knowing God's will.

- God never allows us to live one way and pray another.

- We cannot ask for anything unworthy when we grasp God's holiness.

- God is always deserving of our trust and praise.

- Reverence for God must permeate our whole lives, especially our prayers.

4

DEFINING THE KINGDOM

Mystery: Where is God's kingdom?

Matthew 6:10; Luke 11:2

The woman was a familiar face. People who traveled often saw her peddling vegetables from a cart along country roads. On one occasion a motorist noticed her throwing a stick in the air at an intersection and asked her, "Why are you tossing the stick up like that?"

"I'm trying to decide which road to take," she answered as she continued to toss the stick.

"How many times do you need to throw the stick to decide?"

The woman stopped, turned toward the automobile driver, and said, "Until it points the way I want to go."

Requests Take Wrong Turn

Too often we pray for God's guidance with an attitude identical to the woman described above. Wrong concepts of prayer point us along wrong roads, causing us to lose confidence in the effectiveness of prayer. It happens too often.

Take, for example, the prayers of the Sunday School picnic committee requesting sunshine on the same day that farmers are praying for rain. Barclay puts it in perspective when he suggested, "The correct prayer in such a case is that we should be enabled to enjoy ourselves, hail, rain, or shine."[1] That's an important lesson in the walk of faith.

**The purpose of prayer is not to get our
way, but to get God's will done on earth as
it is in heaven—especially in us.**

The tendency to self-centered prayer is the precise reason Jesus built the petition "Thy kingdom come. Thy will be done in earth, as it is in heaven" (Matt. 6:10, KJV) into His pattern petition. The purpose of prayer is not to get our way, but to get God's will done on earth as it is in heaven—especially in us.

The Kingdom Is Near

When Jesus closed His carpenter's shop and went off to preach, His first message, which He kept repeating, was "The kingdom of heaven is near" (Matt. 4:17). Many rabbis taught that a prayer in which the kingdom is not mentioned is not a true prayer. Bible teacher A. M. Hunter explained: "Every pious Jew in [Jesus'] day prayed in the words of Kaddish, 'May His kingdom be established in your lifetime.'"[2] The Jewish people longingly looked for the coming of Messiah and His reign of peace. Isn't that the ultimate desire of every follower of Jesus, that the Kingdom will come soon, even as it is in heaven?

**The "kingdom" refers to the sovereign rule
of God breaking into human history.**

To keep our priorities straight, Jesus taught us to pray, "Thy kingdom come." The "kingdom" refers to the sovereign rule of God breaking into human history. Jesus leads us to pray, "Thy kingdom come," and then defines "kingdom" as "Thy will be done in earth, as it is in heaven."

Let's go again to my favorite writer, William Barclay, who clarified this issue:

> One of the commonest characteristics of Hebrew style is what is technically known as parallelism. The Hebrew tended to say everything twice. He said it in one way, and then he said it in another way which repeats or amplifies or explains the first way. We then have the perfect definition of the kingdom of God—the kingdom of God is a society upon earth where God's will is as perfectly done as it is in heaven.[3]

The angels in heaven would be just as happy sweeping streets as they would be lighting stars if that is God's command to them. When we pray, "Thy kingdom come. Thy will be done," what are we doing? How do we respond to His directions?

IT'S NOT EASY TO BOW

When Jesus teaches us to pray, "Thy will be done," some human beings react with resentment. Though they may bow to God's will, they don't like to. They would rather have their way and have God quit being God. Others react with resignation. They bow because they have no other option. Such an approach is a passive fatalism, never a Christian virtue.

Jesus would have us react to "Thy will be done" with relinquishment. After all, the One we are asked to obey is our Heavenly Father. He loves us. He is too wise to make a mistake and too good to be unkind. God is worthy of our full trust.

A pastor advised a woman who struggled spiritually, "Tell God, 'Let anything happen to me that You want to happen to me.'"

"Oh, no," she responded. "I don't want that."

I wonder why she fears God.

Missionary E. Stanley Jones explains what I sincerely believe and have seen in my own life and others: "God couldn't will anything for us except our highest good—couldn't and still be God. God's will is our highest interest at all times, in all places, and under all circumstances. Things may happen to us which are not primarily God's will—they come out of the will of man. Their genesis may be evil. And yet, if we let God guide us, He can turn them into good."[4]

That's the kind of God we serve. Check the list again:

- God's will is for our highest good.
- God's will is for our highest interest.
- God's will is for our best in all circumstances.
- God's will is to turn evil into good.

Discover God's Will

To do God's will, we must know what it is. But we will never know the divine will if we are determined to do it our way. For some strange reason, knowing the will of God depends on being willing to do it. Under extreme circumstances, God has been known to reveal His will through a burning bush or a dry fleece made wet or even through an audible voice. But He generally chooses to reveal His will through the Bible.

The Bible is our main sourcebook for discovering God's will. Harry Rimmer reminds us, "Superstitious and casual handling of the Scriptures will not clearly manifest the will of God. There is an old custom which is superstition of the purest order. This consists of shutting the eyes, breathing a prayer, opening the Bible, and stabbing the page with a finger. The technique then is to read the verse of Scripture and follow that as the will of God."[5]

My wife laughs about her parents' idea to name their third son after the first name they found by opening their Bible. Imagine their thoughts as their eyes fell on "Peleg." They named their third son Ray.

Consistent and continuous study of the Bible reveals God's good will for us. Jesus teaches us to pray, "Thy will be done," not "Thy will be changed." How often we would rather tell God how it is—or give Him good suggestions, even while ignoring what He has already told us in Scripture.

My Way or Yours?

A young woman wrote this prayer on her wedding day:

Dear God, I can hardly believe that this is my wedding day. I know I haven't been able to spend much time with You lately with all the rush of getting ready for today, and I'm sorry.

I guess, too, that I feel a little guilty when I try to pray about all this because Larry still isn't a Christian, but oh, Father, I love him so much, what else can I do? I just couldn't give him up.

You know how much I've prayed for him. I've tried not to appear too religious because I didn't want to scare him off. Yet, he isn't antagonistic, and I can't understand why he hasn't responded.

Dear Father, please bless our marriage. I don't want to disobey You, but I do love him and I want to be his wife, so please be with us and please don't spoil my wedding day.

Behind her self-willed rhetoric, here's what she really said: "Dear Father, I don't want to disobey You, but I must have my own way at all costs. I want what You do not want. So, please be a good God and deny yourself, and move off Your throne, and let me take over. If You don't like this, then all I ask is that You bite Your tongue and say or do nothing that will spoil my plans, but let me enjoy myself."[6] I wonder if what we see as being clear about her plea is present in our own ideas about prayer.

God's clear Word would have revealed His will if the young woman had bothered to pay attention: "Do not be yoked together with unbelievers" (2 Cor. 6:14).

God's clear Word would have revealed His will if the young woman had bothered to pay attention: "Do not be yoked together with unbelievers" (2 Cor. 6:14). How could God say it any plainer if the words were written in the sky?

Let's listen to Harry Rimmer again: "It's a sad truth that many Christians read the Bible to find justification for following their own wills. Instead of studying the Holy Word to find God's desire for them, they search for verses that will give them authority for doing what they want to do." He is right.

Rimmer continued by advising, "If you are determined to find a way to have your way, don't bother to pray, 'Thy will be done.'"[7] Before you can effectively pray, "Thy kingdom come," you must first pray, *"My* kingdom *go."* After all, who really is in charge—God or you?

We Must Accept God's Will

Highly respected devotional writer A. W. Tozer pleaded for loving and embracing of God's will: "To will the will of God is to do more than give unprotesting consent to it." That act, he continues, is to choose God's will with positive determination. It means intentionally seeking what God most desires for us.[8] The big question: Do you want what God wants?

The need, then, is to learn to pray, "Thy will be done," with enthusiasm, not "Thy will be endured." The will of God is something to be done joyfully, not to be suffered like a jail sentence or swallowed like a bitter pill.

Frustrated because her five-year-old son refused to swallow a teaspoon of medicine, his mother told him, "Johnny, it's good for you, and God wishes you to take it."

"I'll ask Him," Johnny said as he buried his head under the blankets of his bed and mumbled. Soon a loud, hoarse voice rose from the covers.

"No! Certainly not."

Like the boy, everyone sometimes likes to make up his own version of God's will.

Pastor John MacArthur points out that "the literal Greek of [the petition, 'Thy will be done'] says something like this: 'Your will, whatever You wish to happen, let it happen,' and then the Greek adds, 'As in heaven, so in earth.' In other words, 'God, do what You want.' That is the bottom-line prayer."[9] Trusting the wisdom of God, let's trust His clear words about His will for us as communicated in Scripture.

The Bible gives two vivid contrasts. In the Garden of Eden Adam was saying, "Not Thy will, but mine, be done." In the Garden of Gethsemane, Jesus said, "Not my will, but thine, be done" (Luke 22:42, KJV). There in the garden, in His most bitter struggle, Jesus was really praying the Lord's Prayer again—"Thy kingdom come. Thy will be done in earth, as it is in heaven." He showed us how to genuinely pray well, trusting relinquishment to the full will of God.

Two Words Describe God's Will

The Greek New Testament contains two words to describe the will of God. One word, *boule*, expresses God's irrevocable will, which takes place with or without our consent. For example, God's will in the law of gravity stands whether or not we agree with it. You don't break God's will by defying gravity—you break yourself.

The second word for God's will, *thelema*, carries the idea of desire. God's desire for us can be fulfilled only by our response and acceptance. This second word is found in the Lord's Prayer: "Thy *will* be done" (emphasis added). For God's will to be done, we must accept it freely.

A boy in his father's lap was reading Rom. 12:2: "That ye may prove what is that good, and acceptable, and perfect, will of God" (KJV). He asked his father, "What does the word 'perfect' mean? Does it mean God never makes a mistake?"

Indeed, that is exactly what God's perfect will for you means. God never makes a mistake—what safety and what satisfaction! The Bible assures us about God's will, "Trust in the LORD with all your heart and lean not on your own understanding; in all your ways acknowledge him, and he will make your paths straight" (Prov. 3:5-6). The Lord's Prayer helps us choose to trust our Father.

Referring to the petition "Thy will be done," Archbishop of Canterbury William Temple said, "We have turned what was meant to be a battle cry into a wailing litany." If we trust the Lord, we won't whine about doing His will.

The doctor warned that if the fever didn't drop by morning, death appeared certain.

The wife of Nathaniel Hawthorne wrestled in prayer. Una, their eldest daughter, was dying from malaria. The doctor warned that if the fever didn't drop by morning, death appeared certain.

Nathaniel despaired, saying, "I cannot endure the alternations of hope and fear; therefore, I have settled with myself not to hope at all."

During that long, still night, the mother looked out the window and saw only dark clouds. "I cannot bear this loss— cannot—cannot." Then a thought came to her: "Why should I doubt the goodness of God? Let Him take Una, if He sees best. I can give her to Him. No, I won't fight against Him anymore." She relinquished her child to God.

Mrs. Hawthorne expected sadness at the point of authentic surrender. We all do. But to her surprise, she felt lighter, happier than at any time during Una's long illness. Minutes later, she went into the girl's bedroom to feel her forehead. It was moist and cool. Una was sleeping naturally. A miracle had occurred.

The prayer of relinquishment seeks God's guidance and accepts God's will. I once heard sociologist Tony Campolo say, "It's silly to pray for God's coming rule if I'm not willing to let Him rule over my life now."

IT'S TIME TO ENLIST

As we pray, "Thy kingdom come. Thy will be done," we are enlisting for action. In this petition, we sign up to follow God's plan to use wherever and whenever He desires.

Visualize God's Kingdom

The Bible speaks of God's kingdom as past, present, and future. Underlying all references is the reign of God in the hearts of His people. Wherever and whenever God has been given His rightful place as Sovereign and Lord, the Kingdom already exists.

The Pharisees asked Jesus when God's kingdom would come. He replied, "The kingdom of God does not come with your careful observation, nor will people say, 'Here it is,' or 'There it is,' because the kingdom of God is within you" (Luke 17:20-21). For those who follow Jesus, the Kingdom has come here and now.

Pastor Robert R. Kopp tells the story of a Russian youth who appeared in court for refusing to enter the Soviet Union's army and defended his position by quoting passages from the Bible.

"But my child," the judge said, "that is the kingdom of heaven, and it has not come yet."

"Your Honor," the youth replied, "it may not have come for you, but it has come for me."[10] Have you entered the Lord's kingdom yet?

In a country where social evils are ignored and tiptoed around by the comfortable state church, a minister traveled to several cities with E. Stanley Jones, a powerful evangelist who spoke the truth with kindness and might.

"You preach a very troublesome gospel," the minister observed to "Brother Stanley," as he loved to be called. "We preach a kingdom in heaven, and that doesn't upset anything now. You preach a kingdom on earth, and that upsets everything."[11]

Jesus came to turn the tables on all falsehood. His kingdom builds here and now on the foundations of truth.

Where Jesus Resides

Jesus, however, teaches us to pray, "Thy kingdom come. Thy will be done in earth, as it is in heaven." To visualize the Kingdom, German pastor Helmut Thielicke once wrote, "The kingdom of God is where Jesus Christ is."[12] That idea always inspires me. That's where I want to be—where Christ is.

When Jesus invades us inwardly, we become a part of the Kingdom outwardly. Changes in us affect changes around us. As one Christian testified, "If there were no hereafter, it would be worth it all to have Christ transforming our lives and our homes right now in this world."

Has His kingdom come in you?

How Can a Volunteer Help?

The coming of God's kingdom must begin in each of us. God never forces anyone to accept His kingdom. You must voluntarily choose to accept Jesus' invitation to enter the Kingdom: "I stand at the door and knock. If anyone hears my voice and opens the door, I will come in" (Rev. 3:20). Note that He calls, but we must respond.

> **When we pray, "Thy kingdom come," we are opening our hearts for Jesus to establish His Lordship in us and through us.**

A Chinese Christian was right on target when he prayed, "Lord, revive Your Church, beginning with me." When we pray, "Thy kingdom come," we are opening our hearts for Jesus to establish His Lordship in us and through us. We are committing to be His and to be obedient to Him.

M. S. Rice captured the idea insightfully: "'Thy kingdom come' must not remain merely my prayer; it must become my program."[13] That is the reason this petition is so intensely missionary. No one who is indifferent to the needs of the community and world can honestly pray, "Thy kingdom come." If you are in the Kingdom of light, you can never be content that friends and neighbors are in darkness. God wants us to volunteer as "conscious tools of Providence."

> **No one who is indifferent to the needs of the community and world can honestly pray, "Thy kingdom come."**

Of all the preachers I have heard preach, Louis Evans Sr. is my all-time favorite. He once told the following story.

While an American physician was making a reputation as a surgeon and as a diagnostician, he visited Korea and eventually was called by God to an area where there were thousands of people who had no doctor. After a brief inner rebellion, the physician surrendered to God's call.

During a later visit to Korea, Evans received an invitation from the physician to observe surgeries with Korean medical students in a balcony overlooking the operating table. He said the sun beat down on the roof of that rustic hospital. Ether fumes and the heat drove him out of the room several times. After seven hours, the doctor removed his surgical apron and walked out with Evans.

"Doctor, is every day like this?" Evans asked.

The physician only smiled. Evans noticed that the doctor's forehead was dotted with beads of perspiration, his eyes were weary, his lips purple with strain, and his hands trembled with fatigue.

"How much will you receive for this?" Evans asked as a poor Korean woman was wheeled into the operating room, holding a copper coin in her hand and asking that in Christ's name he give her life.

"Well, sir," the physician replied, "for this I will get nothing but her gratitude and my Master's smile. For that, sir, is worth more than all the plaudits and money the world can give."

Later, Evans said, "I went out of the hospital that day, coming to the conclusion that we are foolish ever to be afraid of Christ's will. We never truly find our lives until first we lose them. To give them away to Christ is to keep them forever."[14]

I have found this true—the path that most frightens us may be the way to blessing and meaning!

You find God's greatest blessings in the place He wants you to be. Pioneer missionary to Africa Harmon Schmelzenbach prayed,

> Lay any burden on me, only sustain me;
> Send me anywhere, only go with me;
> Sever any tie but the one that binds me
> To Thy service and Thy heart.

Let the Lord's Prayer come from your heart as you say it with your lips: "Thy kingdom come. Thy will be done in earth, as it is in heaven." T. W. Manson understood the full implications of the petition when he prayed, "Thy will be done, and done by me." What a satisfying way to pray and live!

Chapter 4

Insights to Transform Your Praying

- "Thy kingdom come" refers to the sovereign rule of God breaking into human history—not only in the past but also in the present.

- Our Heavenly Father is too wise to make a mistake and too good to be unkind.

- To pray, "Thy kingdom come," means we must pray, "My kingdom go."

- If we trust the Lord, we won't whine about doing His will.

- The kingdom of God is where Jesus is.

- To give our lives away to God is to keep our lives forever.

- The path that most frightens us may be the exact way to blessing and meaning.

- "Thy will be done" means to really pray, "May thy will be done in me."

5

GETTING GOD'S WORK DONE

Mystery: What does it mean to pray,
"Thy kingdom come"?

Matthew 6:10; Luke 11:2

Jesus taught His disciples to pray, "Thy kingdom come. Thy will be done in earth, as it is in heaven" (Matt. 6:10, KJV). When thinking of this petition, an unknown writer observed correctly, "Nothing lies outside the reach of prayer except that which lies outside the will of God."

People in our self-serving age, however, appear to pray, "Thy kingdom hold off for a while until my desires are satisfied." Prayer is not an easy way of getting our way, but a significant help to becoming what God wants us to be.

> **So we have the perfect definition of the kingdom of God. The kingdom of God is a society on earth where God's will is as perfectly done as it is in heaven.**

In His Lord's Prayer, Jesus included Hebrew poetic parallelism like what is found in the Psalms: "Thy kingdom come. Thy will be done in earth, as it is in heaven." The second sentence defines the first. So we have the perfect definition of the kingdom of God. The kingdom of God is a society on earth where God's will is as perfectly done as it is in heaven.

How does that work in life? Let's face the fact that our prayers have a way of shaping us and determining our work.

John Owen is absolutely right when he suggested, "He who lives as he ought will endeavor to live as he prays." The question, of course, is "What do we mean and what do we do when we pray, 'Thy kingdom come. Thy will be done'?"

A PRAYER OF COMMITMENT

Praying honestly, "Thy kingdom come. Thy will be done," we commit ourselves to follow God's will and purpose. Such a commitment brings the kingdom of God into the inner world of everyone who honestly submits to the Lordship of Christ. Thus, this prayer of commitment means that we seriously view our responsibilities to God, that His desire is our command. So when praying, we must refrain from giving God suggestions and guidance. Our task is to report for duty.

Billy Graham asked Derek Bok, then president of Harvard University, "What is your students' greatest need?"

Bok thought for a moment and answered, "Commitment."

The same answer applies to Jesus' student-disciples: "Commitment! 'Thy kingdom come. Thy will be done.'" The idea of wholehearted commitment to Christ in our time has to swim upstream against the cultural currents.

A prayer of commitment suggests two things.

Vow to Be Dependable

Every time we pray for God's kingdom to come and for His will to be done, we make a fresh, up-to-date commitment to faithfulness. Does that sound strange to modern ears? I hope not. Missionary David Livingstone didn't think so. On the last day of his life he wrote: "My Jesus, my King, my Life, my All, I again dedicate my whole self to Thee." I like that. In our relationships with God, spouses, and others close to us, we need to make daily commitments—the kingdom of God coming to reality in you.

> **Dependability is a virtue. Too often a person sells out to whims of the moment, while God wants us to build a life that counts.**

Many people make great starts, but Jesus calls us for the long haul. Dependability is a virtue. Too often a person sells out to whims of the moment, while God wants us to build a life that counts.

A faithful pastor illustrated the difference. He said:

> Here are two boys in school. The will of the teacher is that they spend hours in hard studying. One of the boys rebels against the unpleasant work. He wants to be happy, so he goes to a movie. Maybe he quits school altogether to go his carefree way.
>
> The other boy sticks to his studies, difficult though they may be. Look at those same two boys 10 or 20 years later. The carefree boy is now bound and limited by his own ignorance. He endures hardships and embarrassments caused by his lack of training. The other boy is freer, happier, and finds life easier and more rewarding because he was properly prepared.[1]

Dependability pays off in academics, in occupations, in faith development, and in Christian service.

Not an Easy Course

The Lord's Prayer impacts disciples who are students of the Word and students of the will of God. Jesus is not looking for followers who wish only to get by with little commitment or effort. Thus, this prayer rubs against the grain of "easy does it."

An elderly professor at Amherst College began each semester by telling his students, "To you who think you can skim through this course in the same way that you try to skim through all the other courses in this college: I just want to say to you that it can't be done. You will get out of this course exactly what you put into it. And if you put nothing in, that is exactly what you will get out."[2] The Lord's Prayer has little meaning for the person who wants to just "get." But it speaks with strength and courage to authentic disciples of Jesus.

Jesus is talking about a course of discovery and discipline that demands our all-out commitment to Him to the end.

Many churches are filled with people who believe they can skim through with little commitment. They fail to understand what the call of Jesus is about. Jesus is talking about a course of discovery and discipline that demands our all-out commitment to Him to the end. It is really the fulfillment of the reason for which we were created.

Poet Ralph Waldo Emerson spoke to the depth of commitment: "The difference in men is not in their talents but in their dedication." By the same token, we must vow to wholehearted dependability. And we must be expendable as we seek to do the will of God on earth as it is in heaven.

Vow to Be Expendable

Though many people may not realize it, to pray "Thy kingdom come" places them in the position of a patient who is requesting God to perform major spiritual surgery. When we vow to give ourselves totally to God's kingdom, we're talking radical. That word "expendable" conjures up many vivid pictures in our minds.

The first mental picture shows a person given over to a consuming ideal. It is what Lloyd Douglas called a "magnificent obsession."

During the Chinese Civil War, a young Communist lieutenant lived with a captured family between battles. The 19-year-old farm-boy-turned-Communist was about to face a battle in which he knew his odds against survival were 20 to 1.

The Christian man in whose home he stayed said, "Sir, the defending army is better equipped than your army. It is protected by a moat, high walls, and iron gates that are heavily sandbagged."

**Our enemy has no great cause to fight for,
and they will turn and run
when the battle warms up.**

"I know that," he responded, "but our enemy has no great cause to fight for, and they will turn and run when the battle warms up."

"What do you have to fight for?" the Christian asked.

"We are going to change the world in my generation."

"But, sir, it won't do any good if you get killed during your attack on the city tonight."

The young Communist showed the commitment to expendability when he replied, "Chairman Mao has told us we should be willing to die to change the world, and I am quite prepared to die to carry Communism one mile farther."

That's the kind of expendability Jesus had in mind when He announced, "If anyone would come after me, he must deny himself and take up his cross and follow me" (Matt. 16:24).

Capitulate to Christ

The second mental picture of expendability occurred for me when I was a boy and heard a news dispatch during World War II. The transport ship *Dorchester* was torpedoed near Greenland in the early darkness of February 3, 1943. Four chaplains—one Jewish, one Roman Catholic, and two Protestants—gave away their life preservers to save others. As the *Dorchester* sank, those four young men linked arms, braced themselves against the rail, and prayed for the safety of the others. They went down with the ship. That is being expendable.

"Thy kingdom come. Thy will be done" is a petition that vows to capitulate to Christ, to be available for Him and to be expendable by Him. I love the phrase "capitulate to Christ." Too often we capitulate to a thousand lesser causes.

Righting Your Will

One of the great mentors in my life was T. W. Willingham, who loved to debate with me—even until dawn. He helped me see this issue clearly: "One could complain of such a prayer—'thy will be done'—only if he desired something outside of God's will. Only rebellious children and the devil desire anything outside the Father's will." He continued, "When one refuses to pray for the will of the Father, he must feel that his own will is superior to the Father's."[3] I'm quite sure my Heavenly Father is much wiser than I.

Augustine prayed, "Grant that we may never seek to bend the straight to the crooked, that is, Thy will to ours; but that we may bend the crooked to the straight, our will to Thine, that Thy will may be done."[4] Why not stop twisting God's arm to get your way? He is always right.

Somewhere I read that Dwight L. Moody once prayed, "Use me, my Savior, for whatever purpose and in whatever way You may require. Here is my poor heart, an empty vessel. Fill it with Your grace."

In my journal I recorded that British athlete and missionary C. T. Studd observed, "God can do little with those who love their lives or reputations, but there is absolutely no limit to what God can do with men or women who care not whether they live or die so long as they are allowed to fight for Christ and do the will of God."

Methodist Bishop Gerald Kennedy suggests that as we pray, "Thy kingdom come. Thy will be done," we can recite this petition in only one of two positions: "on our knees, saying in confession, 'God be merciful to me a sinner' [or] on our feet, saying in submission, 'Here am I! Send me.'"[5]

A PRAYER OF ENABLEMENT

Kingdom living is here and now and not reserved for "the sweet by-and-by." It's for living in this world, tainted by sin and sinners. The moment we say, "Thy kingdom come. Thy will be done," we are declaring, "Show us, Father, what You can do with us today." Here's good news. We are never left to struggle to do God's will in our own strength. Our Father wants to be our great Enabler.

Depend on God for Everything

Remember we entertain Royalty in residence. Our banner of joy signals that the King lives in residence in our hearts. David sang with exuberance: "Lift up your heads, O you gates; be lifted up, you ancient doors, that the King of glory may come in" (Ps. 24:7). That tune resonates in my heart!

> **As we petition, "Thy kingdom come," we are throwing open the gates of our inner throne room to welcome God's rule in us.**

As we petition, "Thy kingdom come," we are throwing open the gates of our inner throne room to welcome God's rule in us. He enters to govern in power and glory.

Author W. Phillip Keller was born in Kenya, a distant frontier of the British Empire. He recalled the time when Kenyans received the electrifying news that the African colony was to be visited by the king's son, the Prince of Wales.

Everyone was scrubbed, clothes were washed, and shoes

polished. The day arrived, and people exclaimed, "The prince is coming! The prince is coming!" The train carrying royalty rolled into the little station. The place was electric with anticipation.

"Then the prince stepped from the train," Keller wrote. "He established a bit of the British Empire in the soil of Africa. The prince's coming bound the Kenyans to the British crown as no other action could have done."[6]

It's true even more in God's kingdom! We are in the presence of the Heavenly King every time we pray.

Where the King Resides

Our King has come to take up residence in our hearts, not for a visit, but for a permanent relationship. Someone more important than the prince is here. He meets us at the level of our hopes, our limitations, and our infirmities. Having the Lord occupy the throne of our life makes a difference in how we live. We belong to Him, and He is at home in us.

A daughter who had become fed up with unending chores around the house asked her mother, "What kick do you get out of washing dishes that won't stay washed, and making beds that won't stay made, and sweeping floors that won't stay swept?"

"I'm not washing dishes or sweeping floors or making beds only," her mother answered. "I'm building a home for God to show Himself in."[7]

In the same spirit, the prayer "Thy kingdom come" says, "Lord, come on in and make yourself at home here." Remember—God gives himself to us only in the measure in which we give ourselves to Him. Holy Royalty has taken up residence in us.

Make It a Partnership

We have a partnership with Omnipotence. The words express our best intentions: "Thy will be done in earth, as it is in heaven" (KJV). In return God empowers us to accomplish His will. He is a miraculous Partner. I love these two sentences attributed to E. Stanley Jones: "Yourself in your own hands is a problem and a pain. Yourself in God's hands is a possibility and a power." That insight shows how God answers our prayer "Thy will be done." He does it through us.

God's power is given to us in proportion to our obedience. That power is given, not ahead of time, but only as we need it.

Maxie Dunnam gives us an important insight about this partnership with God: "It is only as we act obediently, that the power we need to do what God calls us to do is given. God's power is given to us in proportion to our obedience. That power is given, not ahead of time, but only as we need it."[8]

We supply the person; God supplies the power. Centuries ago Augustine insisted, "Without us, God will not do certain things; without God, we cannot do them." Have you tapped God's resources yet?

Billy Graham's mother schooled her children in the Scriptures. Someone asked her how her famous son could be so effective for God.

"I don't know exactly," she replied, "but I do know this one thing: when Billy gave his life to God, he gave Him all of it." That's an example of exchanging our little for His everything. Being in partnership with God sure makes sense. We give our small self to receive His all—what a bargain!

In struggling to understand how God works in our lives, I am reminded of the advice a saintly Christian wrote to a young missionary: "This is a practical working faith: First, it is a person's business to do the will of God; second, God takes on Himself the special care of that person; third, that person should be afraid of nothing."[9] That kind of confidence in God lifts the load from our shoulders to be shared with the Lord himself.

If you pray for God's will to be done, He will enable you to do His will. D. L. Moody pointed out that "Moses spent 40 years in Pharaoh's court thinking he was somebody, 40 years in the desert learning that he was a nobody, and 40 years showing what God can do with a somebody who found out he was a nobody!"[10] So be patient; God is not finished with us yet. He always can use a "nobody" who is totally yielded to Him.

Be Filled with the Spirit

The great longing in the Church today is the quest for intimacy with God. We are hungry for the inspiration and energizing of the Holy Spirit. For us to entertain Royalty in residence and to enter into partnership with God, we must heed the Bible's command: "Be filled with the Spirit" (Eph. 5:18).

When we rely on His power and not our own, we experience the joy, the fruitfulness, and excitement of the Christian life.

Campus Crusade for Christ President Bill Bright explained these possibilities: "What does it mean to be filled with the Spirit? It means relying on the Holy Spirit in you to change your life, to empower you, and to rely on His power in you to draw others to Himself. When we rely on His power and not our own, we experience the joy, the fruitfulness and excitement of the Christian life."[11] I'm glad the resources are available to us! Let's pray again, "Thy kingdom come. Thy will be done in earth."

A Potter at Work

I borrowed the following life-changing story from W. Phillip Keller. He gives a vivid picture that turns on the light of truth when he introduces an aged craftsman, with deeply lined face and stooped shoulders, who welcomed Keller and his missionary companion to a little, shabby potter's shop.

Keller was reminded of the words from Jer. 18:2 (KJV): "Arise, and go down to the potter's house, and there I will cause thee to hear my words."

The potter led them to a small, dark shed, where they were almost overcome by an "overpowering stench of decaying matter" at the edge of a gaping dark pit in the floor. As the potter's hands brought up a lump of dark mud, it was easy to understand what the psalmist meant: "He brought me up also out of an horrible pit, out of the miry clay" (40:2, KJV).

"Then as the potter gently patted the ugly lump of mud in his hands into a round ball of earth," Keller observed, "I knew God was dealing very plainly with my earthly heart. With meticulous precision, the potter placed the lump of earth exactly in the center of his wheel."

Centering the Clay

Keller continued insightfully, "Just as the potter took special pains to center the clay on the stone wheel, so God exercises very particular care in centering my life down in Christ." He is right—just as the potter molds the mud, so God shapes our lives around our Savior.

I love the way the story unfolds as Keller tells about a fascinating look that crept across the potter's lined face. He says, "Somehow I could sense that in the crude, shapeless fragment of earth between his hands, the potter already saw a vase or goblet of exquisite form and beauty. There was in this clod of crude clay enormous possibilities. The very thought seemed to thrill him."

The Potential in Us

God is our Master Potter who sees what we can become if His will can be done in us. The word picture reminds us of Jer. 18:3: "Then I went down to the potter's house, and, behold, he wrought a work on the wheels" (KJV).

> **Silently, smoothly, the form of a graceful goblet began to take shape beneath those hands. . . . His will actually was being done in earth.**

Let's return to Keller's beautiful account. He continues: "How swiftly but surely the clay responded to the pressure applied to it through those moistened hands. Silently, smoothly, the form of a graceful goblet began to take shape beneath those hands. . . . His will actually was being done in earth."

The stone of the potter's wheel stopped unexpectedly, and the potter removed a bit of grit from the goblet. He started the wheel spinning again and quickly smoothed the surface of the goblet.

"Suddenly he stopped the stone again," Keller said. "He pointed disconsolately to a deep, ragged gouge that cut and scarred the goblet's side. It was ruined beyond repair. In dismay he crushed it beneath his hands, a formless mass of mud lying in a heap upon the potter's wheel."

Wrecked by Resistance

Remember the words of Scripture: "The vessel that he made of clay was marred in the hand of the potter" (Jer. 18:4, KJV). Why was this potential masterpiece ruined in the master's hand? Because the potter encountered resistance.

Keller takes us to the final scene of the drama: "In dismay I turned to my missionary friend and asked in a hoarse whisper, 'What will the potter do now?' The question was passed on.

"The stone started to whirl again. Swiftly, deftly, and in short order a plain little finger bowl was shaped on the wheel. What might have been a rare and gorgeous goblet was now only a peasant's finger bowl. It was certainly second best."

Then Keller asks the searching and searing question we all must ask: "Am I going to be a piece of fine goblet or just a finger bowl? . . . Am I going to be a crude finger bowl in which passersby will dabble their fingers briefly, then pass on and forget all about it?"[12]

How beautifully this story sheds light on one of the most important prayers any disciple of Jesus ever prays:

Have Thine own way, Lord! Have Thine own way!
Thou art the Potter; I am the clay.
Mold me and make me after Thy will,
While I am waiting, yielded and still.
—Adelaide A. Pollard

Because you want to be an effective, beautiful instrument God uses to do His will in the world, why not pray, "Our Father, Thy will be done in earth—in human clay, in me—as it is done in heaven"? God is the Potter, and we are the clay.

Chapter 5

Insights to Transform Your Praying

- Prayer is a significant way of becoming what God wants us to be.

- When we pray, we really report for duty.

- Wholehearted commitment to Christ forces us to swim upstream against the culture.

- Every time we pray the Lord's Prayer, we make a fresh, up-to-date commitment to faithfulness.

- Our enemy has no great cause to fight for, so he will often run when the battle warms up.

- Give up twisting God's arm to get your own way.

- God gives himself to us in the same measure as we give ourselves to Him.

- If God's will is done in your life, it often turns out to be a bit of heaven on earth.

6

ASKING FOR RIGHT THINGS

Mystery: Why should we pray for bread
when it comes from wheat fields?

Matthew 6:11; Luke 11:3

Someone asked Tommy, age five, what he knew about prayer. He answered, "Sure—prayer is asking God for things." Regrettably, such a narrow view of prayer is not limited to little boys. In the Lord's Prayer, Jesus put our request for things in its proper order. He teaches us to acknowledge God as our Heavenly Father, to honor God's name, and to submit to God's will before praying for bread.

Provision for the Present

Only then does Jesus turn His petition and our attention to "asking God for things." He instructed us to pray for needed provisions, pardon, and protection. After all, we do need bread, forgiveness, and guidance. As Pastor John MacArthur suggests, "Bread is provision for the present, forgiveness takes care of the past, and leading takes care of the future."[1] Rejoice in the sufficient provision of God for every period of our earthly journey.

Asking God for things can become complicated in a society directed by bureaucrats. One wag wrote this petition:

We respectfully petition, request and entreat that due and adequate provision be made, this day and the date hereinafter subscribed, for the satisfying of these petitioners' nutritional requirements, and for the organizing of such methods of allocation and distribution as may be deemed necessary and proper to assure the reception by and for said petitioners of such quantities of baked cereal products as shall, in the judgment of the aforesaid petitioners, constitute a sufficient supply thereof.

The Bread of Life

People have a way of cluttering up what Jesus says so simply: "Father, give us daily bread."

> **"Bread" has sometimes been understood in a variety of ways, such as (1) the broken bread of the Lord's Supper, (2) the spiritual bread of God's Word (Matt. 4:4), and (3) as Jesus proclaiming himself to be "the bread of life" (John 6:35).**

That petition sounds so clear, yet throughout church history the "bread" has sometimes been understood in a variety of ways, such as (1) the broken bread of the Lord's Supper, (2) the spiritual bread of God's Word (Matt. 4:4), (3) Jesus proclaiming himself to be "the bread of life" (John 6:35), and (4) the bread of the Messiah's heavenly victory banquet: "Blessed is he that shall eat bread in the kingdom of God" (Luke 14:15, KJV).

The problem springs from the Greek word *epiousios*, translated as "daily" or "daily bread." Our competent commentator friend Barclay understood this Greek word's message as follows:

> The extraordinary fact was that, until a short time ago, there was no other known occurrence of the word in the whole of Greek literature. It was not possible to be sure what it precisely meant. But recently a papyrus fragment was found that was actually a woman's shopping list. And against an item on it was the word, *epiousios*. It was a note to remind her to buy supplies of a certain food for the coming day. . . . This part of the Lord's Prayer is a simple prayer that God will supply us with the things we need for the coming day.[2]

Once again the archaeologist's shovel has uncovered a simply profound biblical understanding. No wonder Origen, a teacher in the Early Church, insisted that "daily bread" be translated as things "necessary for existence." The songwriter catches the meaning so well: "God knows just what I need."

Jesus urges us to pray, "Our Father . . . give us this day our daily bread" (Matt. 6:9, 11, KJV). Consider why this simple petition is so important.

WE CAN'T GO IT ALONE

It's important that we realize our dependency for physical survival on God. Rimmer explained this basic reality: "Our citizenship is in heaven, but we do our eating on earth."[3] The Lord's Prayer shows we have no reason to feel ashamed to pray for our food. In His prayer Jesus shows us that God really cares about our physical needs. God made our bodies, and He wants us to care for them. Jesus never condemned our physical nature as rooted in sin, as the Greeks did.

Physical Needs Are Important

From Jesus' prayer we learn the supreme worth of common things. He never expects us to ignore our natural human desires in some heroic show of spiritual superiority. Asceticism and physical penance do not delight God. Too often they are merely attempts to earn our righteousness. Then these practices turn into cheap substitutes for living by faith in Jesus Christ.

> **Jesus directed a large portion of His ministry, however, to the wholeness of human bodies. We cannot escape our dependency for physical needs.**

People with good intentions sometimes believe they should not pray for physical needs. Jesus directed a large portion of His ministry, however, to the wholeness of human bodies. We cannot escape our dependency for physical needs. I have them, and so do you.

In New Testament Greek, two words stand for "bread." One word, *sîtos*, simply refers to grain-meal bread. In this prayer, Jesus used the other word, *artos*, which represents "bread" in the broader sense of food.

> **Jesus teaches us to pray for food. He knows we don't do well without it for very long.**

In the Lord's Prayer, a prayer uttered by thousands around the world, the term Jesus used for bread covers rice in the Orient, spaghetti in Italy, oatmeal in Britain, tortillas in Mexico, and McDonald's hamburgers and french fries in America. Jesus teaches us to pray for food. He knows we don't do well without it for very long.

Tim Hansel tells the story of Zachary, a two-and-a-half-year-old boy who wanted to pray. His mother had taught him, "Jesus loves me! this I know." It didn't quite come out that way, however, when Zach bowed his head and began, "Jesus loves me—this our toast."[4]

But Zach wasn't far wrong, was he? Prayer for toast fits our common, everyday physical needs. Christians might not always get what they want, but they can expect God to provide what they need. In His extravagant generosity, God often answers Dennis the Menace's prayer, "Give us this day our daily bread—and some peanut butter to spread on it."

Beloved British expositor G. Campbell Morgan said, "I believe that when our Lord teaches us to pray, 'Give us this day our daily bread,' He means all that is necessary for the sustenance of the whole life, physical and spiritual. Jesus never dealt with people in compartments; He always dealt with the whole person."[5] Every essential for living a wholesome, healthy, satisfying life comes to us through the answers God provides to our prayers.

God made our bodies to depend on physical necessities, gave us intelligence to make good use of luxuries, and wisdom enough to know the difference.

The prayer for daily bread seems to suggest necessities, not luxuries. It's prayer for daily bread, not cake. How often we confuse luxuries with necessities! Ancient or modern, we face the same lingering issues. At a fair in Athens, someone asked Socrates what he was thinking. He replied, "How many things there are that I do not need." God made our bodies to depend on physical necessities, gave us intelligence to make good use of luxuries, and wisdom enough to know the difference.

A Daily Need

It's important for every believer to acknowledge dependency on God's resources. Bible teacher J. I. Packer advised that "the prayer of a Christian is not an attempt to force God's hand, but it is a humble acknowledgment of our helplessness and dependence."[6] As we learn to depend on His resources, we can freely and confidently pray for what we need today.

Jesus never forgot the lessons learned from Israel's experience in the wilderness. Nor should we. Remember the story? After the Exodus, Israelis found themselves in the desert country without food. In response to their need, God provided a breadlike substance called manna, which in Hebrew means "What is it?" Obviously He could have given them enough manna to last a long time, but instead, His provisions were fresh every morning. He only gave them enough manna for each day. The Bible says, "Each morning everyone gathered as much as he needed, and when the sun grew hot, it melted away" (Exod. 16:21). In this pattern of provision, God was teaching the people habitual dependence upon Him. He was also teaching lessons about His faithfulness. He knew all of us need to trust God daily for the provisions that sustain our bodies.

Jesus teaches us the same lesson again in the Lord's Prayer: "Give us this day our daily bread." Authentic disciples of Jesus know they are dependent upon our Lord for everything across a lifetime.

> **The father divided the amount into 365 parts and ordered that the portion due should be delivered each day.**

A church leader from an earlier generation, J. B. Chapman, loved to tell about an old rabbi who was asked why God limited His supply of manna to only one day's need. The rabbi explained:

> Once there was a king who made an allowance for his son's support and arranged for the amount to be paid in annual installments. In time it happened that the son arranged to see his father only on the day each year when his gratuity was needed. So the father divided the amount into 365 parts and ordered that the portion due should be delivered each day. After that the son came to his father every day.

The rabbi understood people, himself, and God.

Chapman commented that "if we could get spiritual supplies for an extended period, perhaps we, like the king's son, would forget to come to our heavenly Father for that companionship which is of greater consequence than any detached 'blessing' which could possibly come to us. But our continual dependence will not let us forget."[7] We need close contact with God every moment of every day. And He delights in our coming.

In other words, when we pray, "Give us this day our daily bread," we may really be saying, "Not too much now, lest I forget God later."

A mother of six children stopped frequently at the bakery thrift store. One night she heard her little girl reciting the Lord's Prayer: "Give us this day our day-old bread." God's daily supplies are fresher every day. That makes them enjoyable as well as nutritious.

A Continuing Need

Luke recorded Jesus as saying, "Give us *each day* our daily bread" (Luke 11:3, emphasis added). The grammar of the passage suggests, "Continually give us." I am strengthened by Thomas Carruth's insight: "Each day has a prayer responsibility, and when you fail in prayer one day, you cannot make up for it the following day. You cannot do Monday's praying on Tuesday, and you cannot do Wednesday's praying on Tuesday. Tuesday's praying must be done on Tuesday."[8] Our Heavenly Father delights in daily contact during which we are strengthened by drawing near Him.

Let me borrow a story from Tim Hansel, who tells about a Christian invalid named Sue who was confined to her bed.

"How long must you lie like that?" a visitor asked.

"Just one day at a time," Sue replied.

God doesn't promise help for a month or year in advance, but only for each day: "As thy days, so shall thy strength be" (Deut. 33:25, KJV).[9] That truth applies to all of us.

In 1745 William Williams wrote the hymn "Guide Me, O Thou Great Jehovah." In English, one verse says, "Feed me till I want no more"; but the original line in Welsh says, "Feed me now and evermore." We are now and forever dependent upon the resources of God. And what a joy to know that our generous Father lavishes everything we need on us continually! I enjoy singing the hymn both ways.

COOPERATION COUNTS

God stands ready to answer our petition for bread, but most of the time His answer comes through human cooperation and effort. The formula: We trust God for our daily bread, and He gives us opportunities to earn it. Our prayer is a commitment to cooperate with Him.

Hidden Hand at Work

Our petition for our bread acknowledges that God supplies the food necessary to support our lives. Here in America we live in a prepackaged, reconstituted, frozen, and ready-to-bake society. Because we are so far removed from food sources, we easily forget that in an ultimate sense God provides our food. Without the seed and the sun, there would be nothing to prepackage or freeze.

> **Bless Mommy and Daddy, and give us this day our slow-baked, oven-fresh, butter-topped, vitamin-enriched bread.**

A mother feared that her Tommy had been watching too much television when she heard him saying his prayers: "Bless Mommy and Daddy, and give us this day our slow-baked, oven-fresh, butter-topped, vitamin-enriched bread." Tommy was right, though, because bread always comes from God, who created the soil, energizes the farmer, and provides the sun and the rain to grow the wheat.

God provides our daily food in many ways. Rejoice in His creative extravagance, His matchless laws of nature, and His sustaining force of life that enables our earth to produce harvests. God grants the human family strength and wisdom for planting and caring for the crops that produce the amazing abundance that comes to our tables through the food chain of harvest, manufacturing, and distribution.

In Lystra, Paul preached to the people in the marketplace: "The living God, who made heaven and earth and sea and everything in them . . . has not left himself without testimony: He has shown kindness by giving you rain from heaven and crops in their seasons; he provides you with plenty of food and fills your hearts with joy" (Acts 14:15, 17). It is God who provides for our needs—food for the body and joy for the heart.

Howard Butt tells the story of Sarah, a seven-year-old whose father who was a radio announcer. At a family reunion she was asked to offer the table grace. As members of the clan bowed in reverence, her little soprano voice imitated her daddy's radio charm: "This food comes to us courtesy of Almighty God."[10]

While God doesn't need such commercials, His loving care and His kind hand are behind the process that provides our daily food. Maltbie D. Babcock expresses what we need to hear often:

> Back of the loaf is the snowy flour,
> And back of the flour is the mill,
> And back of the mill is the sun and the shower
> And the wheat, and the Father's will.

God always has a way.

Elijah may have been exiled, but God used the birds to feed him in that lonely place. The poor planning and lack of money of the disciples on the hillsides of Galilee did not stop Jesus from feeding the multitudes. God always has a way. Many of us can testify with the psalmist, "This poor man called, and the LORD heard him" (34:6). I've been there, and God has wonderfully supplied my need. Sadly, world hunger comes from human greed and ignorance and control, while God intends for everyone to have enough to eat in response to the prayer "Give me daily bread."

The Lord Sent It

"Uncle" Buddie Robinson, an early Holiness preacher, experienced times that were hard when preachers weren't popular. His family lived on the prairie outside town.

His wife, Sallie, wrote: "One time we had just enough in the house to eat for one meal. Mammy was out on the porch praying. After a while she came through the house and found a sack of flour on the back porch. Then Mammy had to shout some, and there was great rejoicing in our home. To this day we do not know who brought the flour. But we do know who sent it. The Lord sent it."[11]

The Bible says, "Every good and perfect gift is from above, coming down from the Father" (James 1:17). Let's recognize God's hand at work in the details of our lives, in His provision of food and shelter and clothing.

Work Placed in Our Hands

As the believing Christian lifts empty hands to heaven, God puts work into them. Prayers and labor go together like a horse and carriage or love and marriage. To see God's hands work, we must commit our hands. Much-admired Nazarene church leader R. T. Williams often preached, "Mere prayer does not cook a meal or nail a board where one is needed. But it provides the means so that we may do the cooking and the nailing."[12]

Anyone can bemoan the darkness of a room while praying for an angel to open the windows. But the answer comes when you do your part—get up, open the windows, and help answer your own prayer. I once read this silliness: "The fool smiled and said: 'I shall not plant wheat this year. I will just depend upon fate or Providence. God is too good to let me starve.'"[13] Friends, remember that God is too wise to do for you what you can do for yourself. He gives the energy, the imagination, and the opportunity. He always stands ready to do what you cannot do and to encourage you to do all you can do.

> ### Consequently, the prayer "Give us this day our daily bread" does not promote idleness.

Near the beginning of creation God announced, "By the sweat of your brow you will eat your food" (Gen. 3:19). The New Testament reaffirmed the principle: "If a man will not work, he shall not eat" (2 Thess. 3:10). Consequently, the prayer "Give us this day our daily bread" does not promote idleness. Of course, Jesus taught, "Look at the birds of the air; . . . your heavenly Father feeds them" (Matt. 6:26). A veteran of prayer and good sense said, "God feeds the sparrows, but He doesn't put the crumbs in their mouths." Jesus never encourages idleness. The idea is to pray as if everything depends on God and work as if everything depends on you. That's a winning combination. The Bible says, "If anyone does not provide for his relatives, and especially for his immediate family, he has denied the faith and is worse than an unbeliever" (1 Tim. 5:8).

Watch the birds as they work diligently, flying and flitting from one place to another, gathering here and there. They may pause only to sing a brief song. "Yet your heavenly Father feeds them." And He has at least that much respect for you and for me. The combination is reason for profound thanksgiving. God provides, human beings work, and the process makes us sing.

The World Owes You Nothing

Failure to accept your responsibility in acquiring daily bread contradicts Christian teachings. Some people have been deceived by the false motto "The world owes me a living." An early advocate of the social gospel, Washington Gladden, underscored that truth: "Give us a chance to earn our daily bread by some kind of honest work. We are to eat our own bread. Bread that we beg, steal, cheat, or get by force is not ours."[14]

People who work and earn receive a sense of satisfaction of their daily bread. A cartoon shows members of a family bowing before their meal as the father prays, "Heavenly Father, bless these way overpriced gifts that we are about to receive."

"Give us this day our daily bread" is a prayer of cooperation between God and us. His resources and our labors merge into "our daily bread."

Occasionally we all need to be reminded of the old story about a man who cleared stones, pulled weeds, and enriched the soil of a small farm that eventually produced lovely flowers and vegetables. One evening while the man was showing a pious friend around the garden, the friend said, "It's wonderful what God can do with a bit of ground like this, isn't it?"

"Yes," the man replied, "but you should have seen this ground when God had it to himself."[15] The story is not a put-down of God but an acknowledgment of a divine-human partnership. God prefers being our Coworker instead of our beneficent magician.

GIVE *US*, NOT *ME*

"Give *us* this day *our* daily bread" (emphases added). This is a prayer for the family of God.

"Give *me*" sounds selfish and poverty-stricken. On the contrary, "Give *us*" has the ring of comradeship and relationship. This "us" petition shows that what we ask for ourselves is exactly what we desire for all members of God's family. There's something special about the Lord's people gathering around tables. It has been true in every generation since creation.

On that first Resurrection Sunday, Jesus walked with two people to Emmaus. Though they did not recognize Him, they invited Him to spend the night in their home and to eat with them. Luke described it: "When he was at the table with them, he took bread, gave thanks, broke it and began to give it to them. Then their eyes were opened and they recognized him" (Luke 24:30-31). Jesus was revealed in breaking bread together. His presence was felt. When we meet around a meal where Jesus is present, we are always enriched, and we often discover wonderful new perspectives about God and ourselves.

In the first progress report of the Early Church, the Christians "devoted themselves to the apostles' teaching and *to the fellowship, to the breaking of bread* and to prayer. . . . They broke bread in their homes and ate together with glad and sincere hearts, praising God and enjoying the favor of all the people" (Acts 2:42, 46-47, emphasis added). No meal tastes as good as one eaten in fellowship with the people of God.

A Word of Thanks

The Lord's Prayer shows us that it is important to express our gratitude.

David, age seven, asked his school chum, "Do you say a prayer before you eat?"

"No," he said, "I don't have to. My mother's a good cook."

But David's friend was mistaken, because a good cook is also something for which to be thankful.

God wouldn't teach us to ask Him for food if He had none or not enough to spare.

If we ask God to provide "our daily bread," we should be eager to express gratitude for answered prayer. God wouldn't teach us to ask Him for food if He had none or not enough to spare. Be thankful that our provisions come from our Heavenly Father, who delights in supplying our physical needs.

A pastor went to a notable but crowded eating place in San Antonio. Because men were seated at round tables for maximum use of available space, strangers sometimes ate together. At his table sat a white-haired, suntanned cattleman who was a sincere, simple Christian. The other six fellows at that table bellowed loudly in their struggle for acceptance.

When the food was served, the elderly cattleman bowed his head and thanked God for his food. The other ranchers watched in surprise and winked at each other.

"What's the matter, Pop?" a young rancher blurted. "Have you got a headache?"

"No, sir—my head feels fine."

"You had your eyes shut. Are the lights too bright?"

"No, sir, the light is fine. I was thanking God for my food."

The young man asked, "You don't live in the big city, do you, Pop?"

"No, sir. I live down in the Rio Grande Valley."

"Does everyone down there thank God before he eats?"

We have some who dive right in with both feet as soon as the food is set before them. They never thank God. We call them "hogs" down our way!

With a twinkle in his eyes, the elderly rancher responded, "No, sir. We have some who dive right in with both feet as soon as the food is set before them. They never thank God. We call them 'hogs' down our way!"[16] He then picked up his knife and fork and ate in the loudest silence ever heard in San Antonio.

Please Pass the Bread

"Our Father . . . give us this day our daily bread" is bread we share. This idea reminds me of my longtime friend Reuben Welch's comment. He said, "The bread we receive is bread to share, our daily bread, not my daily bread. We need to pass the bread at God's family table."[17] After all, we are in this Kingdom effort together.

This prayer is not only a prayer that we may receive our daily bread; it is also a prayer that we may share our daily bread with others!

A New Testament commentator who knows life and knows Scripture helps me with this insight: "The problem is not the supply of life's essentials; it is the distribution of them. This prayer [the Lord's Prayer] is a prayer which we can help God answer by giving to others who are less fortunate than we are. This prayer is not only a prayer that we may receive our daily bread; it is also a prayer that we may share our daily bread with others!"[18] That's another dimension of the "us" prayer.

Writer Howard Snyder, who is so committed to the social dimensions of the gospel, put this "us" prayer in perspective: "It is not wrong to have three meals a day and a roof over our heads. But what does Jesus think about those who have no roof over their heads and no meals any days?" And what does God want us to do for them?

Snyder then offered a clear Christian point of view: "I become very uncomfortable when I hear Christians saying that since God has promised to give us 'the desires of our hearts' we should therefore expect all kinds of 'material blessings' from God. We may come to think that an ever-rising, middle-class standard of living is a kind of guaranteed minimum wage of the Christian faith, something that goes along with salvation."

If we think this means Christians are to live like royalty in a starving world, then we should go back to the New Testament and take another look.

Then Snyder clearly underscores the pressing issue: "The theological implications of such a view are staggering. God is King, but if we think this means Christians are to live like royalty in a starving world, then we should go back to the New

Testament and take another look at the Jesus who preached the Kingdom."[19] When we do, we soon see that a prosperity gospel does not fit in every nation and culture of the world. Therefore, it is a false gospel.

As a Hindu in India was lecturing with eloquence about his religion, he was distracted by the cries of hungry children begging for bread outside the window. He suddenly got up, walked to the window, and closed it, shutting out the cries that interrupted his beautiful talk about religion. Christians sometimes do the same thing in their hearts or in the details of their conduct.

Christians Feed Others

Hear this sobering word from Evangelist C. William Fisher:

This petition that Jesus taught His disciples to pray makes that kind of callous indifference impossible. For to even be His disciple means that one not only hears the cries of the weak and hungry and lost but is compassionate enough to share with those who are needy.

Real Christians don't close their hearts, or their eyes, or their checkbooks. They open their doors and their pocketbooks and their compassion to those less fortunate. For they know that no matter what they have, they are not owners, but stewards, and stewards will one day give an accounting of their stewardship.[20]

Stewards always have a day of accounting, a day of joy for the faithful steward and a day of dread for the unfaithful steward.

The lessons of the "give us our daily bread" part of the prayer are impressive and grand and demanding too. With a sense of dependency, an attitude of cooperation, and the responsibility of community, let's learn again what it really means to pray, "Our Father . . . give us this day our daily bread." Please pass the bread.

Chapter 6

Insights to Transform Your Praying

- In the Lord's Prayer, bread is for the present, forgiveness cares for the past, and the divine leading cares for the future.

- Jesus addressed a large part of His earthly ministry to wholeness and wellness of the human body.

- The prayer of the Christian is not to force God's hand but to accept His will.

- God delights in our coming to Him in prayer.

- Our prayer for bread involves a commitment to cooperate with God in providing for that bread.

- Recognize the hand of God in all the details of your life.

- God is too wise to do for you what you can do for yourself.

- Like an earthly father, God delights in supplying our needs.

7

DUMPING TRASH BASKETS

*Mystery: Why would God care
about my sins or trespasses?*

Matthew 6:12; Luke 11:4

The Methodist and Presbyterian congregations in a small town worshiped together during the summer. They moved between sanctuaries over three months. For the sake of harmony, the worshipers used whichever form of the Lord's Prayer that was traditional for the host congregation. At the final service of the summer the minister announced, "The time has now come for the Methodists to return to their 'trespasses' and leave the Presbyterians to their 'debts.'"[1]

I love the story of a four-year-old child who prayed, "Forgive us our trash baskets as we forgive those who fill our trash baskets." Her confusion of "trespasses" with "trash baskets" is quite understandable and reminds me of a Mayor's Prayer Breakfast in Spokane, Washington, in which the concluding event was the unison recitation of the Lord's Prayer. The huge audience intoned the familiar phrases of the prayer, but much mumbling and hesitation drowned out the words "trespasses" and "debts." The resultant sound really did sound like "trash baskets." Perhaps trash baskets is the real issue.

Because Matthew's account records, "Forgive us our debts" (6:12), and Luke wrote, "Forgive us our sins" (11:4), the common contemporary use of "trespasses" made me curious. It turns out that William Tyndale, in his early English translation, for some unknown reason used "trespasses," which was later adopted in the liturgy by editors of the Church of England's *Book of Common Prayer.* "Trespasses" is a mistranslation.[2]

But after we have discussed and endlessly rehashed the use of the words "trespasses," "debts," and "sins," we are left with the need to empty trash from our lives. We need to confess our need of God's forgiveness frequently. As the old country preacher proclaimed, "We need to tattle on ourselves to God."

Father Stands Watch, and He Knows Us

Whether we pray, "Forgive us our debts" or "Forgive us our sins," we are seeking forgiveness from "Our Father . . . in heaven." In the day before discipline was called "child abuse," a boy flagrantly broke the rules of his family. Consequently, his father sent him to spend the night in the barn. The youngster felt so guilty over grieving his father that he tossed and turned restlessly. He was also frightened and lonely. Around midnight he heard someone climbing the ladder to the hayloft.

"Are you sleeping?" his father asked.

"No, Dad," the boy responded.

"I can't sleep either," the father confessed. "I'm not changing my mind about right and wrong, but I've come to sleep with you. I'd like to share the punishment with you. Move over, Son, and put your head on my arm. Let's get some sleep."

That boy found forgiveness in the personal presence of his father.

> **The good news is not that I can go
> to heaven, but that my God will
> be there when I arrive.**

Certainly it is good news to know we are forgiven by God, but the greater discovery is to know that God is a forgiver. I pass on to you what blessed my heart: "The good news is not that the Judgment is coming, but that our Father is the Judge. The good news is not that I can go to heaven, but that my God will be there when I arrive."[3] Think of it: our Heavenly Father—the One whose name we hallow—is a forgiver. In the Lord's Prayer, Jesus teaches us important lessons about God's wholehearted forgiveness.

FORGIVENESS IS BASIC

Having petitioned "Give us this day our daily bread," Jesus adds, "*and* forgive us" (emphasis added). Our Lord links our need for food with our need for forgiveness. One is as urgent as the other. God's forgiving is fully as generous as His giving of material provisions. In His foresight God knew that we would need food—and that we would need forgiveness. Forgiveness is among humankind's deepest need and God's highest provision.

When we pray, "Give us daily bread," God's hand provides adequate resources. When we pray, "Forgive our debts or sins," God's heart provides amazing forgiveness. Forgiveness is a basic need for everyone all the time. John MacArthur quoted a hospital administrator: "I could dismiss half my patients tomorrow if they could be assured of forgiveness."[4] God's forgiveness is the first step to spiritual and emotional wholeness. For us all, forgiveness is only a prayer away.

Psychologists Agree

During a Billy Graham crusade in Honolulu, a university sent 20 psychologists to critique the proceedings. In reports to the newspapers, the psychologists agreed on one thing: Graham's call for people to repent and to receive God's forgiveness was psychologically sound. People need to be forgiven.

United States Senate Chaplain Lloyd Ogilvie told about a sick woman who underwent a series of tests and expected some wonder drug would be prescribed to cure her illness. Although the doctor's prescription was not a wonder drug, it was a miracle cure that simply said, "Your future happiness depends on being forgiven and forgiving."[5] Forgiveness is like that. It provides wholeness and wellness of the mind, body, and spirit.

FORGIVENESS IS ESSENTIAL

Jesus taught us to pray, "Forgive *us*" (emphasis added). It appears He directed this prayer to His followers, not to unconverted sinners. As disciples of Jesus, we must pray for forgiveness to keep our relationship with God unclouded and our relationships to others unbroken. With our lists of prayer requests tightly in our hands, does it occur to us to ask for God's forgiveness?

**Let no one imagine himself able to reach
the point during this earthly life where he
will no longer have need of forgiveness.**

Great Reformer Martin Luther understood human beings thoroughly when he said, "Let no one imagine himself able to reach the point during this earthly life where he will no longer have need of forgiveness. If God did not ceaselessly pardon, we should be lost."[6] We thrive on His forgiveness.

Pastor Myron F. Boyd concluded, "We believe that even the best of Christians constantly need the atoning blood to cover mistakes, faults, weaknesses, sins of omission or sins of commission. 1 John provides us with clear teaching. God's standard is that the Christian should not sin. God's provision is that if one should sin, he has an Advocate (defense lawyer) with God the Father, even 'Jesus Christ the Righteous.'"[7] Jesus is on our side, and He has provided forgiveness.

What Must We Do?

A Sunday School teacher asked, "What must we do before we can receive forgiveness of sins?"

One student responded, "We must sin!" The human family is good at that, but Jesus came along to forgive us of sin. To receive God's forgiveness, we must confess our need and pray, "Forgive us."

**Too many moderns are like the man in a
cartoon who is standing in the doorway
while the church secretary tells the
pastor, "Says he wants to confess his
neighbor's sins."**

To recognize our need of forgiveness we must have an accurate sense of sin. Too many moderns are like the man in a cartoon who is standing in the doorway while the church secretary tells the pastor, "Says he wants to confess his neighbor's sins."

God's continuing forgiveness is essential for every child of God. By His forgiveness we are kept up-to-date in our relationship with God. The Bible clearly teaches, "If we claim to be without sin, we deceive ourselves and the truth is not in us. If we confess our sins, he is faithful and just and will forgive us our sins and purify us from all unrighteousness" (1 John 1:8-9). If we agree that our sins separate us from God and we confess our need, God is quick to rebuild His relationship with us.

In the old Anglo-Saxon language, the word "forgiveness" was "forth giving." It referred to something you give away, something that passes from your hand. God offers us complete restoration. The governor of our state can officially pardon a thief, but the man is still a thief. When God forgives a thief, however, He transforms him into an honest man. God's forgiveness restores even as it makes us willing to forgive others.

In his book *Prayer That Prevails*, G. Ray Jordan tells the story of a woman who doubted that God could forgive her but declared, "If He ever does forgive me, He will never hear the last of it."[8] Let's not be so tight-lipped, having enjoyed God's forgiveness through Jesus Christ; let's celebrate and rejoice about the forgiveness He has provided.

As we pray the Lord's Prayer during public worship, someone always needs divine forgiveness. Even though people may not admit it openly, their hearts hunger and thirst for God's pardon.

Jesus knew we need to pray openly and often, "and forgive *us*" (emphasis added). Great London pastor of another era Leslie Weatherhead wrote, "The forgiveness of God, in my opinion, is the most powerful therapeutic provision in the world."[9] That's how the Lord restores our spiritual health.

FORGIVENESS IS PROVIDED

Jesus taught us to pray, "And forgive us our *debts*" or "our *sins*" (emphases added).

In this relationship, we need to understand the enormity of our obligation to God. His grace is never to be taken for granted.

God's Laws Broken

Most likely Jesus spoke the original Lord's Prayer in Aramaic, the language of Babylon. In the Aramaic language the word *hobha* means "debt" or "sin." Writing for Jewish readers who were often meticulous in good deeds, Matthew translated *hobha* into Greek as "debts." Writing for Greek readers, Luke translated *hobha* as "sins." Gentiles had flagrantly, unashamedly broken God's laws.

> **An unfulfilled responsibility was a debt unpaid. In the Greek of the New Testament, "debts" (opheilemata) were failures to render to God His due, a "failure in duty."**

"Our debts" involve sins of omission. The Greek word translated "debts" was a term used in courts of law as damages awarded in a lawsuit. Jewish teachers commonly used "debt" for "responsibility." The idea is similar to our legal term "liability." An unfulfilled responsibility was a debt unpaid. In the Greek of the New Testament, "debts" *(opheilemata)* were failures to render to God His due, a "failure in duty." Who can claim to have fulfilled paying all that is due God?

German Pastor Helmut Thielicke said in an inspiring sermon, "In the gospel, generally the terms 'guilt' and 'debt' are understood not so much in the sense of an active breach of God's command, but rather as something that I owe and have not paid, something I have neglected and omitted."[10] "Shortcomings" is the word used in Weymouth's translation. J. B. Phillips's paraphrase: "What we owe to you."

Our sins of omission cannot be ignored. As Thielicke reminds us, Jesus will someday say: "You did *not* feed me, you did *not* give me a drink, you did *not* visit me when I crossed your path in the person of your hungry, imprisoned, lonely human brother. You owe me food, clothing, drink, attention." He continues, "Do you remember the person you noticed because of the sadness that lay on his face, the person who was waiting for you to say a word to help him on his way?"[11] Too often we are guilty of neglect. So we need to pray, "Our Father . . . forgive us our debts." We mean our blindness, our oversight, and our omission of what we could have done.

Missing the Mark

"Our sins" involve sins of commission. Luke employs the Greek word *hamartias* for sins, the most common New Testament word for sin, which means "missing the mark." The matter of motive or intention is important in discussing sins of commission.

Harold Walker reminds us of something we might like to forget: "Anybody can be forgiven for missing the mark, but to miss the mark and then to insist you hit it until you make yourself believe you did is unforgivable."[12]

The subtle insistence on doing one's own thing needs God's forgiveness, His eraser that removes ugly blots from the pages of the past.

Hamartia describes a person's actions that are off target from God's will. Such sins occur in those incidents when the Christian acts rebelliously or independently of God's known will. A self-directed life is off target from a Spirit-filled life. The subtle insistence on doing one's own thing needs God's forgiveness, His eraser that removes ugly blots from the pages of the past.

God's forgiveness is needed for socially acceptable sins: riding roughshod over people's feelings, gossiping, spreading malicious slander, betraying trust, robbing God's tithe to spend on yourself, rejecting unlovable people, disrupting the unity of Jesus' Church, and disobeying the clear Word of God.

Our sins of omission and sins of commission combine into an enormous debt we owe to God, which needs divine forgiveness.

We have no means by which to balance the debts of our moral failures.

In these issues we must face bankruptcy of our merit. George Bernard Shaw has a character in one of his plays say, "Forgiveness is a beggar's refuge. . . . We must pay our debts." Unfortunately, Shaw apparently did not understand that we cannot pay our debt because we have no moral assets. We have no means by which to balance the debts of our moral failures. As one of my favorite hymns says, "Were the whole realm of nature mine, / That were a present far too small" (Isaac Watts). We cannot pull ourselves up by our own bootstraps when we have no boots.

Works Won't Work

We can't work off our account with God. The Bible says, "God our Savior . . . saved us, not because of righteous things we had done, but because of his mercy" (Titus 3:4-5). Our only hope for canceling our enormous debt can be found in God's mercy and forgiveness.

> **If I were only 50 percent kind and 75 percent pure in heart yesterday, there's no way I can make it up by being 150 percent kind and 125 percent pure today.**

We can do nothing to make God love us more than He already does. We are bankrupt, insolvent, infinite debtors. That keeps us totally dependent on His mercy. If I were only 50 percent kind and 75 percent pure in heart yesterday, there's no way I can make it up by being 150 percent kind and 125 percent pure today.

There's no free lunch. Somehow someone must always pay the penalty for bad conduct. We live in a moral universe that demands justice. The good news of Jesus is that God through Christ has borne the cost. He has paid the penalty for our sins. We can do nothing but gratefully receive the forgiveness God offers in Jesus Christ.

Paul H. Hetrick of Siteki, Swaziland, wrote:

A missionary related how the culture of the people with whom she works is permeated with the concept of what she called "pay back." It is expected that there be a pay back for everything from intentional insult or injury to the smallest kindness shown. Accidental deaths caused by a second party are paid back by a reciprocal killing. Some sort of pay back is expected even for so-called gifts. . . .

The forgiveness which flows from the Cross meets, and must melt, our narrow human understanding of forgiveness if we are to grasp what God is saying to us through His Son. . . .

This concept of forgiveness is beyond the grasp of our finite thinking. The Cross says, "It's yours." But like the prodigal son, we cry out, "I am not worthy—just let me do something, and then I won't feel so bad about accepting it. 'Make me as one of your hired men'" (Luke 15:19, NASB).

But the Father says, "No. There can be no pay back. Just accept it."[13]

We are deeply indebted to our Father in heaven, who has made a way for our restoration from moral and spiritual failure.

Impossible Debt Forgiven

We need to recognize the full extent of our forgiveness. Jesus told a mind-boggling story about a king settling accounts with his subordinates. One man owed the king about $20 million. Brought before the king and threatened with slavery, the fellow begged, "Be patient with me . . . and I will pay back everything" (Matt. 18:26). The king knew it was an impossible debt, so he canceled the entire amount.

> **Although he had heard the word "forgiven" pronounced, he failed to comprehend the reality of his total forgiveness.**

Immediately following the forgiveness of his $20 million debt, the man sent one of his debtors to jail because he owed him approximately $20. Obviously the fellow never comprehended the enormity of his own debt nor the enormity of his forgiveness. Although he had heard the word "forgiven" pronounced, he failed to comprehend the reality of his total forgiveness.

Satan can hold us hostage as he tries to convince us, "You aren't worthy. You deserve to be unhappy. You aren't good enough." In spite of God's complete provision for sin, Satan tries to flash close-up scenes on the screens of our memories depicting our sins and bad attitudes that merit God's judgment. When you are forgiven, you are truly and completely forgiven.

> **Some Christians struggle from one anxiety to another, plodding through fogs of doubt and dread, convinced that they can never be good enough to win God's smile of approval.**

Some Christians fearfully go through life troubled, insecure, bouncing from one exaggerated problem to the next, from one imaginary threat to another in an awful effort to punish themselves. They struggle from one anxiety to another, plodding through fogs of doubt and dread, convinced that they can never be good enough to win God's smile of approval.

Their image of God is a shriveled, stern, demanding mockery of our God of love and mercy. To them, His forgiveness is a fragile, fickle thing that flimsily covers our sins, only to shrink when soaked with tears of regret.

Beware of Satan's Taunt

Satan's accusation of inadequate forgiveness makes us lose confidence in the future and in God's mighty works of grace. But God's answer is eternally adequate—Jesus. He is always better to us than we deserve.

Bible scholar John Stott wrote, "Sin is likened to a 'debt' because it deserves to be punished. But when God forgives sin, He remits the penalty and drops the charge against us."[14]

The Lord declares, "I will forgive their wickedness and will remember their sins no more" (Jer. 31:34). What a promise and what relief! As Pastor John MacArthur explains, "Forgiveness is taking away our sin, covering our sin, blotting out our sin, and forgetting our sin."[15]

The Bible says, "You are a forgiving God, gracious and compassionate, slow to anger and abounding in love" (Neh. 9:17). God eagerly forgives and forgets. The Bible assures us. "You . . . delight to show mercy" (Mic. 7:18). All this means we don't have to coax God to forgive us but to simply call on His name and to confess our indebtedness.

Monk Finds Refuge

Missionary John T. Seamands wrote that on the morning of July 6, 1962, "My heart literally burned within me" while reading a news story headlined, "Monk Hanged as Assassin." The Associated Press story reported that T. Somarama, a Buddhist monk, had been hanged for the assassination of an Asian prime minister in 1959.

Seamands continued, "Prison officials said Somarama was baptized as a Christian 24 hours before the hanging so that he could ask for the forgiveness that the Buddhist religion does not grant.

Only when he turned to the One who died in his place on the Cross could he find the deliverance for which he longed.

"Here was a Buddhist who felt the weight of his crime and the guilt of his sin but could find no solace in his own religion. Only when he turned to the One who died in his place on the Cross could he find the deliverance for which he longed."[16]

That's the kind of God we have in Jesus. His forgiveness is complete. Having been forgiven, we can keep right on walking with Jesus. As veteran pastor Charles Allen observed, God doesn't want us to "keep on confessing the same sin. He doesn't want us to keep chewing over the past."[17] God wants to forgive us of our sins and for us to separate ourselves from all acts of wickedness and unrighteousness.

Don't Rub Your Nose in Sin

Do you keep doing perpetual penance? Are you letting Satan continually rub your nose in past sins and failures? Confess them and leave them at the cross of Jesus. Accept His sacrificial death on the Cross as sufficient for all sin. Jesus is God's Provision for our sins. That's tremendously good news!

One of Papa's rules with his children was to settle whatever wrong we had done before we went to bed.

Charles Allen illustrated God's attitude toward our confessed sins by telling of his own father: "One of Papa's rules with his children was to settle whatever wrong we had done before we went to bed. If we needed talking to, he never put it off until tomorrow. After the matter was settled, he never mentioned it again, nor would he permit us to."[18] That's God's pattern too. He forgives and forgets.

David, the shepherd-king, sang, "Praise the LORD, O my soul, and forget not all his benefits. . . . He does not treat us as our sins deserve or repay us according to our iniquities. For as high as the heavens are above the earth, so great is his love for those who fear him; as far as the east is from the west, so far has he removed our transgressions from us" (Ps. 103:2, 10-12).

Bruce Larson told a story of a respected man in the community who operated a feed and grain store during the Great Depression. He extended credit to so many customers who were unable to pay that he eventually was forced to declare bankruptcy. It took him many years to repay all the liens against his business.

On the day his last creditor was paid, the elderly gentleman took his books, including all the records of the people who still owed him money, and burned them in a huge bonfire. In that grand act of forgiveness, he released the debts of all those people. He himself bore the awful burden of debt, and each debtor was completely forgiven and free.[19] That's just like Jesus.

Sin Nailed to the Cross

The Bible says: "God made you alive with Christ. He forgave us all our sins, having canceled the written code, with its regulations, that was against us and that stood opposed to us; he took it away, nailing it to the cross" (Col. 2:13-14). Jesus bore the burden of our debts and sins. Though the Christian intends to serve the Lord faithfully, each of us has need to pray, "And forgive us our debts."

The apostle John understood our predicament when he wrote, "My dear children, I write this to you so that you will not sin. But if anybody does sin, we have one who speaks to the Father in our defense—Jesus Christ, the Righteous One. He is the atoning sacrifice for our sins, and not only for ours but also for the sins of the whole world" (1 John 2:1-2).

Let no unconfessed debt or sin keep you from enjoying God's complete and continuing forgiveness. Don't hesitate to pray, "And forgive us our debts."

On the Cross Jesus cried out, *"Tetelestai!"* (John 19:30). In marketplace Greek that means, "Paid in full!" And it is.

Chapter 7

Insights to Transform Your Praying

- God's forgiveness may be the greatest news in the world.

- Forgiveness is the most basic human need between God and us.

- God's forgiveness is the first step toward spiritual and emotional wholeness.

- Your future happiness depends on being forgiven and forgiving.

- To recognize our need for forgiveness, we need a serious sense of sin.

- Our sins of omission and commission combine to make us owe God an enormous debt.

- Try to understand the completeness of your forgiveness.

- God is always better to us than we could ever deserve.

8

FORGIVENESS IS CONDITIONAL

Mystery: How can God's forgiveness be limited to me?

Matthew 6:12; Luke 11:4

As the Sunday School children prayed, a small boy said, "Forgive us our debts, as we forgive those who are dead against us." That's another way of saying, "Forgive us our debts, as we forgive our debtors" (Matt. 6:12, KJV).

As We Forgive

The Lord's Prayer teaches us the important lesson that God's forgiveness is conditional: "Forgive us our debts, *as we forgive* our debtors" (emphasis added). Jesus does not infer that we earn our forgiveness by forgiving others, but His forgiveness is so incredibly complete that it motivates us to forgive completely.

There's a great difference between praying, "Forgive us *because* we forgive," and "Forgive *in the same way as* we forgive." Matthew's Greek word order enlightens: "and forgive us the debts of us, as indeed we forgave the debtors of us." In this petition Jesus binds "forgiving" and "forgiven" together forever. They cannot be separated.

Perhaps Jesus emphasized forgiveness because it is so easy to say but so difficult to give.

The petition on forgiveness is the only one that Jesus emphasized and expanded. After finishing the Lord's Prayer, He immediately commented: "For if you forgive men when they sin against you, your heavenly Father will also forgive you. But if you do not forgive men their sins, your Father will not forgive your sins" (Matt. 6:14-15). Perhaps Jesus emphasized forgiveness because it is so easy to say but so difficult to give.

When we ask for forgiveness, we are promising to give up all known sin, especially the sin of hate or resentment. It is impossible to expect God to make you a new person in Christ while you keep your heart full of hate. The Bible is so clear and so insistent about giving forgiveness. "We know that we have passed from death to life, because we love our brothers. Anyone who does not love remains in death" (1 John 3:14). Receiving forgiveness is conditioned on giving forgiveness.

FORGIVE OTHERS

"Only one petition in the Lord's Prayer has any condition attached to it—the petition for forgiveness." According to William Temple, though it may come as a surprise, unconditional forgiveness is foreign to the Bible. Though God's love is unconditional, His forgiveness is conditional. The phrase "as we forgive our debtors" is better translated, "as we have forgiven." That means a completed act.

After a person belongs to the family of God, he or she must operate within the principles of God's kingdom.

A person outside the kingdom of God may ask to be forgiven of all sins committed. Out of God's unconditional love, that person receives total forgiveness. But after that person belongs to the family of God, he or she must operate within the principles of God's kingdom.

A child of God receives forgiveness for sins of omission and sins of commission in the same way that he or she has forgiven others. Robert R. Kopp is right: "Lots of folks don't like this prayer. Let's face it. If they did like it, things would be a lot better at home, down on the job, or wherever." He continues,

"Lots of folks prefer to hate each other. Even way back in the late fourth and fifth centuries, Chrysostom reported that churches were deleting this part of the prayer because they couldn't believe that God's forgiveness is conditional upon a forgiving spirit within the person seeking His pardon."[1] Keep in mind this prayer belongs only to followers of Jesus. For others it rubs against the grain of selfishness.

Avoid Closing the Door

If you say or think, "I'll never forgive you," you cannot receive God's forgiveness. If you are not willing to forgive others, you are not ready to be forgiven. An unforgiving spirit shuts the door on God's forgiving grace. You can surround yourself with an unforgiving attitude and completely block yourself off from the forgiving mercy of God.

It's not that God cannot forgive the unforgiving person, but the unforgiving person is incapable of receiving forgiveness. *The Broadman Bible Commentary* accurately notes, "When a door is closed, it is closed from both sides. What blocks the flow of mercy or forgiveness *from* us blocks its flow *to* us."[2] Jesus said, "Blessed are the merciful, for they will be shown mercy" (Matt. 5:7).

The governor of the Georgia colony, General Oglethorpe, was reported to have said to missionary John Wesley, "I never forgive!"

"Then, sir, I hope you never sin, since if you sin you will stand in need of divine forgiveness," Wesley replied.

On this exact point William Barclay insists that "if we refuse to forgive others, we are asking God not to forgive us. If we pray this petition with an unhealed breach, an unsettled quarrel in our lives, we are asking God not to forgive us."[3]

Beware of the Liar's Trap

Unforgiving is unforgiven. We can't ask God to do for us what we refuse to do for others. The Bible states, "If anyone says, 'I love God,' yet hates his brother, he is a liar. For anyone who does not love his brother, whom he has seen, cannot love God, whom he has not seen" (1 John 4:20).

My seminary professor Mendell Taylor suggested that people excuse themselves by saying, "I'm just human, and I have feelings. You don't know what they said, you don't know how they treated me, and you don't know what attitude they took."

If you want to be forgiven by your Heavenly Father, you have to be forgiving.

But that is not the question. "If you want to be forgiven by your Heavenly Father, you have to be forgiving. You cannot control what the other person does or says, but you can determine what your attitude is going to be. . . . 'Forgive me, Father, as I forgive.'"[4] What a Christlike way of living!

In an old *Amos 'n' Andy* radio program, Andy became fed up with a big man who slapped him across the chest every time they met.

I put a stick of dynamite in my vest pocket, and the next time he slaps me he's going to get his hand blown off.

"I'm fixed for him," Andy tells Amos. "I put a stick of dynamite in my vest pocket, and the next time he slaps me he's going to get his hand blown off."[5] That makes us chuckle until we remember the dynamite of *hatred* may wound someone else while destroying us.

Sangster and Davison underscored how unforgiveness works: "Some people nurse a resentment for years. They do not realize that every time they say the Lord's Prayer it becomes a bitter blasphemy, searing and shriveling their own souls. He who refuses to forgive has severed the spiritual artery by which the life of God flows into the soul."[6]

Jesus knew people like us pretty well when He said, "And when you stand praying, if you hold anything against anyone, forgive him, so that your Father in heaven may forgive you your sins" (Mark 11:25). Here's the healthy point: I refuse to allow some dumb thing somebody did to me to hinder my enjoyment of God's full and free forgiveness. In fact, forgiving someone else may be a favor you give yourself.

EVENING THE SCORE

The impact of the prayer is clearly "Cancel our debts as we ourselves cancel the debts of our debtors." Its literal meaning says, "Forgive us . . . in proportion as we forgive." No evening of the score allowed.

If I pray, "Forgive us," I am praying, "Forgive me and forgive the person whom I hate." I can pray that way only if I am seeking to resolve the conflicts I have with another "in proportion as we forgive."

Lloyd Douglas in his powerful novel *Magnificent Obsession* introduced us to a student named Dawson who is bitterly out of sorts with his professor and the school's dean.

"I'm going to tell him I'm through and that they can all go to hell," he says.

"That would be a great blunder, Dawson," his friend Bobbie replied. "They might go, and where would that leave you? You see, my son, every time you send a man to hell with whom you have had close personal contacts, he takes a part of you along with him. And then some fine day, when things are ever so much better with you, and you need to contact all there is of your scattered personality for some noble purpose, a considerable chunk of you is missing, and you have to go to hell after it."[7]

I'm much better off forgiving others than getting even.

Prayers That Go Unanswered

To refuse to forgive is a passive vow to get even. That means that as you pray the Lord's Prayer, you are really asking God to get even with you.

> **God never chooses to answer prayers that are filled with bitterness and resentment.**

For years a woman had prayed for her husband, who had committed adultery, to become a Christian. Nothing happened, perhaps because she had not forgiven him. She felt wounded, though spiritually superior. God never chooses to answer prayers that are filled with bitterness and resentment.

While living in the South Pacific, Robert Louis Stevenson conducted family worship each morning and always concluded with the Lord's Prayer. One morning he got up and walked out of the room. When his wife asked what was wrong, Stevenson replied, "I am not fit to pray the Lord's Prayer today." Such self-evaluation should be ours every time we pray the Lord's Prayer.

Apparently Stevenson had been savoring some resentments against someone. He had indeed disqualified himself to pray, "Forgive us our debts, as we forgive our debtors." The solution to such a spiritual deadlock is to forgive others.

Make Things Right Today

Jon, a 13-year-old boy, came home from school with a black eye he had suffered in a fight. His mother wisely said, "Tonight and tomorrow will be very difficult if you don't make it right today. I want you to call the boy you fought with and apologize."

"Aw, Mama," the boy said. "It was his fault. He hit me first."

"Jon, it will be one of the hardest things you've ever done, but I want you to call now and say that you're sorry about the fight."

Hi, Bill. It's Jon. I'm sorry about the fight. Can we still be friends?

Jon, his shoulders slumped, held an ice pack over his eye as he reluctantly followed his mother's advice. A few minutes later he greeted his buddy with a loud, enthusiastic "Hi, Bill. It's Jon. I'm sorry about the fight. Can we still be friends?"

With friendship renewed, Jon hung up the phone, hurried to the kitchen, and opened the door to the refrigerator.

"What's to eat, Mama?" he asked. Jon had personally experienced the joy of giving forgiveness to someone who had offended him.

It's powerful, wonderful work.[8]

The Jews of Jesus' day had a saying that no man should lie down in his bed without forgiving everyone who had offended him. Such a practice makes it possible for us to pray, "And forgive us our debts, as we forgive our debtors."

FORGIVEN BY FORGIVING

One sure sign of our own forgiveness shows up in our willingness to gladly forgive all who have sinned against us.

Skeptically a man asked, "What good did God do for Stephen when the angry mob stoned him?"

As Joseph Parker, a turn-of-the-century London preacher, suggested, God enabled Stephen to pray, "Lord, do not hold this sin against them" (Acts 7:60). That's a mighty step forward in Christlikeness. Our capacity to forgive other people shows that we have experienced God's forgiveness.

A woman's friends treated her badly. Her inner world seethed with resentment. A Christian friend pointed her to Jesus, who can offer the gift of forgiveness. They prayed together, and she asked God to forgive her of such deep resentments. When she got up from her knees, her face shone as she said, "A great load has been lifted from my heart. Now I can go out and forgive others." Just now remove from your life anything that hinders your forgiveness of others.

A Reflection of Discipleship

Our reactions to others always show the quality of our discipleship to Jesus. The Bible is clear in its expectation, "Let no debt remain outstanding, except the continuing debt to love one another, for he who loves his fellowman has fulfilled the law" (Rom. 13:8). What a demand and what a blessing it provides! Keep on praying, "Forgive us our debts, as we forgive our debtors"! My friend Paul Martin advised and lived, "Forgiveness is the language of heaven. We'll need it to get there. We'll have to forgive others to enjoy heaven."[9]

Charles Colson told of two young men on a platform before a huge gathering of Protestants and Catholics. Liam, a Catholic, had been the last member of the Maze Prison hunger strikes in Ireland that took the lives of nearly a dozen IRA terrorists. Liam had starved himself for 55 days until his mother persuaded him to break his fast.

> **Through his witness for Christ, Jimmy, a Protestant terrorist, came to know Jesus.**

Afterwards Liam gave his heart to Jesus Christ. God's love enabled him to forgive the people he once hated. Through his witness for Christ, Jimmy, a Protestant terrorist, came to know Jesus. Now they stood side by side at the International Conference of Prison Fellowship in Belfast, Northern Ireland.

In his powerful testimony, Liam put his arm around Jimmy's shoulders and said, "Before, if I had seen Jimmy on the streets, I would have shot him. Now he's my brother in Christ. I would die for him!"

God's forgiveness is life-changing.

British Bible expositor Martyn Lloyd-Jones wrote, "Whenever I see myself before God and realize something of what my blessed Lord has done for me at Calvary, I am ready to forgive anybody anything. I cannot withhold it. I do not even want to withhold it."[10] That's the motive for giving forgiveness.

When we stop forgiving, we stop growing spiritually. There may be tears, heartbreak, and struggle, but God flows His forgiving love through us and enables us to forgive others. Jesus said, "Freely you have received, freely give" (Matt. 10:8). Unforgiveness may be the biggest hindrance to Christian growth.

Forgiving: an Act of Will

Leo Buscaglia, professor at the University of Southern California, said, "Forgiving is an act of will. It is a volitional choice. We either choose to forgive or we do not."[11] Many Christians believe they cannot forgive until they feel like it. Nonsense— you can choose to forgive whether you feel like it or not!

Jesus said, "If your brother wrongs you, go and have it out with him at once—just between the two of you. If he will listen to you, you have won him back as your brother" (Matt. 18:15, PHILLIPS). Notice the instruction does not provide for a dozen detours to tell your friends how badly you have been treated.

We must mean it when we pray, "Forgive us . . . as we forgive." Novelist George Herbert understood the issues clearly: "He who cannot forgive destroys the bridge over which he himself must pass." The greatest bridge-builder of all time hung on the Cross, looked down the corridor of time, and prayed, "Father, forgive them, for they do not know what they are doing" (Luke 23:34). It's still true. Most of the people who wrong us do not know what they are doing.

The history of art provides us a great example. While Leonardo da Vinci was painting his famous portrayal of *The Last Supper,* he had a quarrel with an acquaintance. Revengefully, he painted an unmistakable likeness of his enemy on the face of Judas, reasoning that the face of Judas would make his enemy an object of derision for as long as the painting lasted.

Later, however, when da Vinci came to paint the face of Christ, he was unable to paint the likeness he desired. Everything seemed to go wrong. Again and again he tried, but the portrait of Jesus never turned out satisfactory. In his heart da Vinci knew the reason—his resentment toward his enemy.

Finally he painted out the face of Judas, went to his rival, and was reconciled. Only then was the artist able to portray the face of Jesus.

We will never be able to show the likeness of Jesus in our lives until we forgive those who hurt and wrong us. We mar the image of Jesus until we forgive the faces of our "debtors."

Nazi Guard Forgiven

Forgiving is hard, demanding work. Corrie ten Boom survived Hitler's concentration camps. She was tough and held up under brutality, but Corrie's sister was frail and sickly. Corrie couldn't tolerate the physical, mental, and psychological abuse inflicted on her sister. One particular Nazi guard was exceptionally cruel to both of them. Finally her sister died from the torture. Tremendous resentment built up in Corrie.

> **Resentment, bitterness, and hurt swelled within her as she recalled the terrible memories of her sister being tortured and abused.**

Long after the war, God sent Corrie to Germany with the message of forgiveness. At the end of a service one night while she was greeting the people, shaking their hands as they were leaving, she suddenly looked up into the eyes of the man who had been their Nazi tormentor. Resentment, bitterness, and hurt swelled up within her as she recalled the terrible memories of her sister being tortured and abused. Though the man didn't recognize Corrie as an ex-prisoner, she knew him.

"Corrie, I was a guard in a Nazi concentration camp," he said. "I've tortured people, some even to death. But I've become a Christian. God has forgiven me. I've come here tonight

because I need to know I have been forgiven by your people."
He lifted up his hand and asked, "Will you forgive me?"

With all that resentment, bitterness, and hurt bottled up,
Corrie couldn't raise her hand and put it in his. Inwardly she
cried to God, "O God—help me. Give me strength." No sooner
had she prayed than her hand settled in his hand. She looked
into the man's eyes and said, "I forgive you." Little did he
know the extent to which she forgave him, but Corrie said later,
"I was set free at last!"

"And forgive us . . . as we forgive"!

**When you forgive someone, you set a
prisoner free. Then you find out
the prisoner is you.**

A neighboring pastor's wife, Shirley Bertholf, once told my
congregation, "When you forgive someone, you set a prisoner
free. Then you find out the prisoner is you." The Bible says,
"Therefore, as God's chosen people, holy and dearly loved,
clothe yourselves with compassion, kindness, humility, gentle-
ness and patience. Bear with each other and forgive whatever
grievances you may have against one another. Forgive as the
Lord forgave you" (Col. 3:12-13). Let's forgive to help others for
our own good and for Jesus' glory. Forgive not in measured
amounts, but extravagantly "forgive as the Lord forgave you."

Chapter 8

Insights to Transform Your Praying

- Forgiveness from God is conditioned on our forgiveness of others.

- Hatred may wound someone else, but it destroys the one who
  hates.

- God never answers prayers that are filled with resentment or
  selfishness.

- Forgiveness is the language of heaven.

- When we stop forgiving, we stop growing spiritually.

- If your brother or sister offend you, go to him or her at once.

- It is Christlike and smart to forgive others rather than to get even.

- Forgiving is an act of the will.

9

UNDER NEW MANAGEMENT

Mystery: Is God really in charge of the universe?

Matthew 6:13; Luke 11:4

A youngster in the big city wondered why he was taught to pray, "And lead us not into Penn Station." Another boy misquoted the prayer by saying, "But deliver us from eagles."[1] Children, however, are not the only ones puzzled by this petition in the Lord's Prayer.

After teaching His disciples to pray for forgiveness and to give forgiveness, Jesus joins the last petition with a significant "and"—"And lead us not into temptation." With sins of the past resolved, Jesus now turns our attention to the future. We must understand two issues before analyzing this petition:

1. God does not entice us with evil. The Bible is clear in its teaching that "God cannot be tempted by evil, nor does he tempt anyone" (James 1:13). God is not the author of evil. Let's get the facts absolutely straight: God is not the tempter, but He is the Deliverer.

The poetic emphasis focuses on God's deliverance from evil.

2. This part of the prayer is also formed in Hebrew poetic thought. The words "Lead us not into temptation" are a poetic negative statement in contrast to the much more positive statement, "Deliver us from evil" (KJV). The poetic contrast in He-

brew would say, "Give us not darkness, but light." The poetic emphasis focuses on God's deliverance from evil. Adam Clarke, contemporary to John Wesley, helped us when he said, "God is said to do a thing which He only permits to be done."[2] In other words, if God permits something, some people are quite sure it was His creation. That means if I am tempted, then I blame Him for it. But that's not the kind of God we serve.

> **This phrase of the Lord's Prayer, "And lead us not into temptation," is our heart's cry that God will lead us as He led David.**

This last petition of the Lord's Prayer expresses the longing of God's children for holiness, for Christlikeness, and for deliverance from anything that mars Christ's image in them. David rejoiced about what he had learned from experience: "He leadeth me in the paths of righteousness for his name's sake" (Ps. 23:3, KJV). This phrase of the Lord's Prayer, "And lead us not into temptation," is our heart's cry that God will lead us as He led David.

This last petition of the Lord's Prayer teaches us three important lessons about Christian living and about our praying.

TEMPTATION IS REAL

Jesus viewed evil as reality, not as some quaint illusion. He spoke of evil as a grim fact of life, and He aligned himself against it. Evil is real.

Two Classes of Evil

Natural evil. We call catastrophes like earthquakes, floods, tornadoes, and diseases "evil" because they destroy human life. The same catastrophic event on some distant, empty planet would not seem evil. Such events are simply violent processes of change in nature. Only to the extent that such things inflict suffering do we apply the term "evil."

> **God rarely chooses to suspend the natural workings of this universe even to reward believers.**

Prayer never guarantees that natural evil will bypass you. Jesus says that our Father in heaven "causes his sun to rise on the evil and the good, and sends rain on the righteous and the unrighteous" (Matt. 5:45). God rarely chooses to suspend the natural workings of this universe even to reward believers.

Don't expect automatic immunity from natural evil. Don't become discouraged when God does not choose to suspend the laws of nature for your benefit. God does not take hailstones out of the sky or falling rocks out of the road just for us.

However, in spite of natural evil we can trust our Heavenly Father. Threatened to be thrown into that fiery blast furnace, Shadrach, Meshach, and Abednego proclaimed with confidence, "The God we serve is able to save us from it. . . . But even if he does not, we want you to know, O king, that we will not serve your gods or worship the image of gold you have set up" (Dan. 3:17-18). That confidence works in natural evil fully as well as it does in evil caused by wicked people like the king.

Moral evil. The rebellious spirit of man resides at the heart of moral evil. Moral evil is personal. Freedom to do right also means freedom to do wrong. Thus, temptation can easily lead to the terrible cancer of rebellion against God. Jesus teaches us to pray for protection against moral evil: "And lead us not into temptation, but deliver us from evil" (KJV).

Two Meanings of Temptation

Temptation may be a test to develop character. The Greek word *peirasmos* is a neutral word that suggests "test, proving, or trial." Our Father knows we need testing for spiritual development. Thus, He does not shelter us from all temptation but allows it for our strengthening.

Barclay's explanation helps us understand this kind of temptation. He says, "Temptation is not designed to make us sinners. It is designed to make us good. We may fail in the test, but we were not meant to. We were meant to emerge stronger and finer."[3] God's plan is not to protect us from discomfort but to make us stronger. He would rather make us holy than happy. Old Testament Joseph explained this idea to his brothers, who had sold him into slavery decades earlier: "You intended to harm me, but God intended it for good" (Gen. 50:20).

Therefore, Jesus was teaching us to pray, "Do not allow us to be overcome by our testing." Or to put it positively, "Use our temptations to make us strong." We never outgrow our need for being tested so that we may enjoy spiritual growth. Peter wrote about our trials: "These have come so that your faith—of greater worth than gold, which perishes even though refined by fire—may be proved genuine and may result in praise, glory and honor when Jesus Christ is revealed" (1 Pet. 1:7).

Temptation may be an invitation to commit sin. This meaning of temptation is never ascribed to God. He sent us Jesus to save us from the power of sin. Note the incredible differences. A test seeks to bring out the best in us; a temptation to sin seeks to bring out the worst. Giving in to a temptation to sin destroys our faith and ruins our life.

Often people wrongly assume they are developing moral resistance by exposing themselves to the allure of sin. That's always dangerous. We never completely outgrow the threat of sin's seduction. A young man asked an old priest, "Father, when will I cease to be bothered by the temptations of the flesh?"

The priest replied, "I wouldn't trust myself, son, until I was dead three days." That's good advice!

Sources of Temptation

Temptations may come from within. Down inside we seem to like temptation. Could it be that we don't really want to get completely rid of sin but to be free from its consequences? One fellow's sweatshirt explains the dilemma: "Lead me not into temptation—I can find it myself."

Beware of weak spots. An insightful commentator observed, "In everyone . . . is some weak spot; and at that weak spot temptation launches its attack. The point of vulnerability differs in all of us. What is a violent temptation to one man leaves another man quite unmoved."[4] What stirs you up?

An overweight fellow decided to shed some excess pounds. Taking his diet seriously, he even changed his route to work to avoid his favorite bakery. Then one morning he came to work with a big coffee cake.

**I prayed, "Lord, if You want me to
have one of those delicious coffee cakes,
let me have a parking place directly
in front of the bakery."**

"This is a very special coffee cake," he explained. "I accidentally drove by the bakery this morning, and there in the window were a host of goodies. I felt that was no accident, so I prayed, 'Lord, if You want me to have one of those delicious coffee cakes, let me have a parking place directly in front of the bakery.' And sure enough, the eighth time around the block, there it was."

We sometimes act that way too. What is your favorite temptation—I mean the one to which you are most friendly?

Beware of strong points. We may guard against our weaknesses, but we often take chances with our strengths. Scripture warns us, "So, if you think you are standing firm, be careful that you don't fall!" (1 Cor. 10:12).

**History is full of the stories of castles which
were taken just at the point where the
defenders thought them so strong that
no guard was necessary.**

One Bible teacher helpfully suggested, "We are in the habit of saying, 'That is one thing . . . I would never do,' [and] it is just there that we should be upon the watch. History is full of the stories of castles which were taken just at the point where the defenders thought them so strong that no guard was necessary."[5] Friends, be alert and watchful, and keep your eyes on Jesus!

Temptations may come from without. Temptations can spring from our social environment or circumstances of life. We need to pray, "And lead us not into temptation." Circumstances, relationships, and unusual situations can all bring us temptation.

Attacks can come from the left, like poverty, illness, marriage difficulties, problems on the job, and people whose influence drags us down. We sometimes stagger under one blow of circumstance after another. Then we may begin to doubt God's goodness and mercy. At those times we especially need to pray, "Lead us not into temptation."

Eventually we become arrogant or self-righteous, and in the end we even believe that we deserve our good fortune.

Attacks can come from the right. A false sense of security, acquisition of wealth, successful careers, good health, good reputation, recognition by people who love us are some danger points. Prolonged streaks of good fortune can set you up for danger. Bible student Walter Luthi explains how this problem develops: "Eventually we become arrogant or self-righteous, and in the end we even believe that we deserve our good fortune. We stop being grateful and begin to savour the most splendid gifts as if they were a foregone conclusion."[6] Does God really owe you smooth sailing? Probably not.

A Greek youth was holding the tiller of a small boat in the Aegean Sea as an old sailor told a story. Absorbed in the conversation, the youth had to be reminded to be more careful with his steering. He replied in innocence, "The following wind is favorable."

The old sailor smiled and said, "It is just for that reason that the danger of going off course is so great."

Yes, we must resist attacks from the right when everything seems favorable by praying, "And lead us not into temptation."

Attacks may come from below. The devil himself tempts us. Paul warned, "Put on the full armor of God so that you can take your stand against the devil's schemes" (Eph. 6:11). Apparently the enemy of our soul plans his worst attacks for those who are most determined to get closer and closer to Christ.

The Bible does not think of evil as an abstract principle or force, but as an active, personal power in opposition to God.

Alan B. Stringfield uncovers the devil's worst scheme: "Satan's best and most unique work is to convince people that he doesn't exist."[7] Barclay is faithful to Scripture when he wrote, "The Bible does not think of evil as an abstract principle or force, but as an active, personal power in opposition to God."[8] Behind evil is "the evil one."

It's time to remember and to tell everyone that our help from above is more powerful than any attack from within, from without, or from below. Temptation is real, but victory is always possible through the enabling nearness of Christ.

FAILURE IS POSSIBLE

Temptation is not sin; it is the yielding that is sin. Jesus himself was tempted, yet He refused to yield to it. We are not marred by temptation, only by sin. Remember the old story about applicants for a chauffeur's job? The person looking for a safe driver asked applicants, "How near the cliff's edge are you skillful enough to drive?"

One fellow replied, "Within a foot."

A second said, "Within six inches."

Pat, an Irishman, responded, "I'd keep as far from the edge as possible just to be safe." Pat got the job, and he has an important lesson for us—"Keep as far from the edge as possible just to be safe."

Jesus would rather you walk with Him as far from the edge as possible.

Why bother to live as close as you can get to temptation? Jesus would rather you walk with Him as far from the edge as possible. Temptation may be inevitable, but embracing, welcoming, and yielding to temptation isn't.

Steps That Lead to Defeat

Temptation is always the first step to defeat and sin. If the possibility of failure did not exist, then the temptation would have no power and have no attraction to us. But let's remember temptation usually comes through a door that has been left open deliberately.

1. We can be overconfident about a particular temptation. Charles Allen tells about a reformed alcoholic who had apparently conquered his drinking habit. Quite overconfident, when he came to town he hitched his horse to the familiar hitching post in front of the town saloon. He was victimized eventually by the old temptations. "Had he had a healthy fear of temptation, he would have changed his hitching post."[9] Don't flaunt or be overconfident about temptation.

2. We can allow desire to capture our interest. This can be done by cultivating wrong friends or feeding your mind a wrong mental diet. The first frame of a "Hagar the Horrible" cartoon showed a sign outside a church advertising a sermon on "The Six Worst Sins in the World." The next frame showed a packed house of drooling church attenders.[10] Don't allow yourself to be teased by temptations. Run from them.

3. We can allow temptation to seduce us. One author titled a sermon on this part of the Lord's Prayer, "When Bad Things Taste Good." Temptation seeks to stimulate some present desire. Although I've never been tempted to eat turnips, I know other areas of life in which I must deny temptations immediately. When we begin to toy with or welcome a temptation, we are in trouble. Then we play with it, and its appeal increases. That's a dangerous fix, even though we may enjoy it.

> **Too often we pray this prayer and then flirt with passion and tease with sin as though we were strong and the devil were a weakling.**

I once heard the prayer paraphrased like this: "Keep us in the testing time, save us from playing with evil, keep us from attractions that will be too much for us." Too often we pray this prayer and then flirt with passion and tease with sin as though we were strong and the devil were a weakling. He's not.[11]

The apostle Paul gives excellent advice regarding resisting temptation. He wrote, "Whatever is true, whatever is noble, whatever is right, whatever is pure, whatever is lovely, whatever is admirable—if anything is excellent or praiseworthy—think about such things" (Phil. 4:8). What you think is what you become.

4. We can flirt with temptation. The Bible clearly advises us, "A man's temptation is due to the pull of his own inward desires, which greatly attract him. It is his own desire which conceives and gives birth to sin" (James 1:14-15, PHILLIPS). We can will to do God's will or will our own way. Jesus' pattern in the wilderness temptation provides the way to victory.

5. The last step is an attempt to hide spiritual defeat.
Usually we follow one of three choices.

We act as though nothing happened. Thus, we try to keep up a religious facade, though the peace, joy, and presence of Jesus are gone. Denial never frees the sinner.

We make excuses. At this point we blame others, especially the devil. Some blame people who have been in the cemetery for years. What pitiful self-delusion!

> **Often we give new names to old sins. What has been proclaimed as the "new morality" is simply the old immorality dressed in a new vocabulary but still filled with the old decay.**

We adjust our values to include the wrongdoing. Often we give new names to old sins. What has been proclaimed as the "new morality" is simply the old immorality dressed in a new vocabulary but still filled with the old decay.

There is good news, though: *Any temptation that defeated us does not have the final word.* The way to recovery starts with confession of sin. The Bible assures us of full recovery: "If we confess our sins, he is faithful and just and will forgive us our sins and purify us from all unrighteousness" (1 John 1:9). That's genuine forgiveness. The apostle John emphasized the same truth in these powerful words: "My dear children, I write this to you so that you will not sin. But if anybody does sin, we have one who speaks to the Father in our defense—Jesus Christ, the Righteous One. He is the atoning sacrifice for our sins" (2:1-2).

Jesus wants us to pray, "Lead us not into temptation, but deliver us from evil." Temptation is really real. Don't be fooled. Failure is a genuine possibility. But there is more to the story of God's redemption and grace.

DELIVERANCE IS AVAILABLE

Missionary Evangelist E. Stanley Jones had good insight when he wrote this petition with the following punctuation:

"And lead us, not into temptation, but deliver us from evil." I have inserted the first comma, which is legitimate, because no punctuation appeared in the original. That changes the sense. The prayer is for leading: Lead us.

The rest points to where the leading should be: "not into temptation, but from evil." This portion of the prayer is hardly morally intelligible without the punctuation, for God cannot lead us into temptation. . . . "Lead us, so that evil is not a temptation to us any longer."[12]

A Brief, Powerful Petition

The prayer "Deliver us" literally means "Save us." This means "Break our chains." What a powerful prayer! Many Bible prayers are brief, to the point, and desperate. Peter cried, "Lord, save me!" (Matt. 14:30), and He did. The poor mother simply asked, "Lord, help me!" (15:25), and He did.

Jesus heard them both, and He hears us. Brief prayers can be incredibly effective. As little Freddy started falling out of a tree, he cried, "Lord, save me! Save me!" There was a pause, and then he said, "Never mind, Lord—my pants just caught on a branch." Sometimes we are like that without recognizing who has charge of the branch.

> **This petition from the Lord's Prayer, "Deliver us from evil," seeks deliverance from all moral evil and freedom from sin's domination. It seeks divine help so we may be at our best.**

This petition from the Lord's Prayer, "Deliver us from evil," seeks deliverance from all moral evil and freedom from sin's domination. It seeks divine help so we may be at our best. Jesus taught us to expect deliverance. The biggest lie of the devil is that we have to sin. "After all, you are human," he argues in an attempt to get us to quit the struggle.[13] Of course, we are human and tempted, but because of Jesus we can enjoy deliverance.

Our Father not only can restore us but also can protect us. In an old-time camp meeting, a former homeless alcoholic told how God had saved him out of the gutter. Someone else who had served time in prison related how God had rescued him from a life of crime. After several people testified to the power of God to deliver them from terrible sin, Gypsy Smith jumped up and fairly shouted, "The Lord has done great things for you, but He has done far greater for me. He saved me from going astray. He has kept me from my youth."[14] Deliverance means we can be freed from the deepest sin—and also we can be protected from the deepest sin.

Safety Net Is Available

An incredibly reassuring biblical benediction begins, "To him who is able to keep you from falling and to present you before his glorious presence without fault and with great joy" (Jude 24).

Here the Bible tells us deliverance is needed. The prayer "Deliver us from evil" concedes that only God's power can save us. The Bible says it so clearly: "Salvation is found in no one else, for there is no other name under heaven given to men by which we must be saved" (Acts 4:12). We cannot deliver ourselves. Like a frightened child, we turn to God. As Blaise •
Pascal exclaimed, "I hold out my arms toward my Liberator."

Here the Bible tells us deliverance is guaranteed. "God is faithful; he will not let you be tempted beyond what you can bear. But when you are tempted, he will also provide a way out so that you can stand up under it" (1 Cor. 10:13). That means for even the most severe temptation, God provides power for you to overcome it.

> **We can never excuse ourselves by saying, "It was too much for me." The Bible promises God will always provide a way out.**

God's promise of deliverance has never been repealed. That means you never have to give in, regardless of the enormity of your temptation. We fail only because we choose to do so. We can never excuse ourselves by saying, "It was too much for me." The Bible promises God will always provide a way out.

At the end of World War II Bruce Larson was stationed in Germany where sins of the flesh beckoned constantly. In those circumstances he prayed, "Lord, I am Your person now. I don't want to be a part of this scene, but I'm weak." He reminded the

Lord of His promise: "He will not let you be tempted beyond what you can bear." He prayed, "Lord, I claim that promise." And he said it worked.[15]

Every believer can do the same thing. In keeping with God's promise, pray, "Don't allow me to be tested beyond my limits."

The Bible tells us that deliverance is complete. Jesus promises, "Lo, I am with you alway" (Matt. 28:20, KJV). Jesus is always present and available to us. The Synodale Version used in French churches translates this last petition: "Abandon us not to temptation."[16] God never abandons us.

During the Korean War a young soldier burst into the chaplain's tent: "Chaplain, pray for me. We jump off in an hour. Pray that I will come back alive."

> **I can't ask God to favor you more than He does other soldiers. But I tell you what I *will* do—I'll go with you.**

After calming the fellow, the chaplain said, "Son, I can't offer that kind of prayer. You are going out where the grenades will be bursting and the bombs falling. Hell is going to break loose. Some are not coming back. I can't ask God to favor you more than He does other soldiers. But I tell you what I *will* do—I'll go with you."

That's what our Lord does for us. He does not whisk away all of our temptations, but He promises to go with us—all the way home, even when the way leads through the bombs, the grenades, and the hells of life.

God Provides Wisdom

After introducing the subject of trials and temptations, the apostle James advises us, "If any of you lacks wisdom, he should ask God, who gives generously to all without finding fault, and it will be given to him" (James 1:5). What a promise! God endows us with a sanctified common sense to help us avoid unnecessary temptation. Paul urged young Pastor Timothy concerning temptation, "But you, man of God, flee from all this" (1 Tim. 6:11). Flee temptation and don't leave a forwarding address.

We Have a Holy Helper

The Holy Spirit strengthens us for everything we face. Hear this promise: "I pray that out of his glorious riches he may strengthen you with power through his Spirit in your inner being" (Eph. 3:16). And God answers that prayer. The Holy Spirit equips us so we may "resist the devil, and he will flee from you" (James 4:7).

The Holy Spirit equips us so we may "resist the devil, and he will flee from you" (James 4:7).

Someone suggested, "What makes resisting temptation difficult for most people is that they don't want to discourage it completely." But let us pray boldly, "Deliver us from evil."

While traveling, a Russian Communist official saw a peasant kneeling in the middle of a field praying. He stopped his car, stomped over, and said, "You waste your time like this instead of plowing and planting for the party."

"But, commissar, I'm praying for the party."

"Praying for the party? And years ago you probably prayed for the czar."

"I did, commissar."

"Well, look what happened to him."

"Right."

The Bible supports such prayer. "For God did not give us a spirit of timidity, but a spirit of power, of love and of self-discipline" (2 Tim. 1:7). Our Father has equipped us with everything we need to overcome temptation.

The Word Is Our Defense

Jesus did not offer Satan a list of reasons why He shouldn't concede to his temptations. Instead, our Lord answered every attack by quoting Scripture. That's the Christian's security system.

A lonely teenager sought advice from Mother Gibson, who at 80 sparkled with the presence of God. The teen asked, "How can I handle this particular temptation?"

Why, honey girl, temptation is just another name for the devil. When the devil bothers me, I read the Bible to him.

"Temptation?" Mother Gibson replied. "Why, honey girl, temptation is just another name for the devil. When the devil bothers me, I read the Bible to him."

"You what?" exclaimed the girl.

Mother Gibson picked up her Bible and held it high. "I tell him, 'Temptation, you old devil, all the promises in this Book are mine. See that? Read it.' Then I read it to him and say, 'You just skedaddle on out of here.' Try this. It works."[17]

The Word of God is a strong defense. But we must *use* God's Word as *our* Defense. Scripture advises us, "I have hidden your word in my heart that I might not sin against you" (Ps. 119:11).

Let's face facts: Temptation is real. Failure can happen. Sin is a present possibility. But deliverance is available, possible, and provided. It's comforting to know that our Deliverer is "our Father." To Him we address this prayer: "Our Father . . . lead us not into temptation, but deliver us from evil."

It makes me feel like the child who was enjoying a trip on a transatlantic ocean liner, even during a terrible storm.

"Aren't you afraid?" a passenger asked.

"No, sir," the lad replied. "My father is the captain."

Our Father has everything under control if we rest ourselves in Him.

On the night of an Indian male's 13th birthday, having learned hunting, scouting, and fishing skills, he was given a final test.

Early American Indians had a unique practice for training young braves. On the night of an Indian male's 13th birthday, having learned hunting, scouting, and fishing skills, he was given a final test. Braves placed him in a dense forest to spend the entire night alone. The experience was horribly frightening. Until then, he had never been away from the security of his family and tribe. But he was blindfolded and taken several miles away on this night.

When he took off his blindfold, he found himself in the middle of a thick woods. He felt terrified. Every time a twig snapped, he visualized a wild animal ready to pounce. After what seemed like an eternity, dawn broke, and the first rays of sunlight began to lighten the forest. Looking around, the boy saw flowers, trees, and the path out of the woods.

Then, to his amazement, he saw a man standing nearby, armed with bow and arrow. It was his father, who had been there all night. That's our experience too.

When the dark night of your temptation lifts, you will find that your Heavenly Father has been there all the time. He proves to a skeptical world through you that "greater is he that is in you, than he that is in the world" (1 John 4:4, KJV).

Chapter 9

Insights to Transform Your Praying

- Though temptation is real, it is not sin until we consent to it.

- Everyone is tempted, but the issue is what you do with it.

- Prayer does not guarantee that natural evil will bypass you.

- Freedom to do right also gives us freedom to do wrong.

- Temptation often comes as a test of our character to strengthen us.

- Deliverance from any temptation is possible through the power of God.

- Temptation sometimes comes at the point of our greatest strength.

- Satan plans his worst attack for those who are most determined to live close to Christ.

10

ALL GOD'S PEOPLE SAY . . .

Mystery: What does "Amen" mean?

Matthew 6:13, KJV

Throughout these conversations about the Lord's Prayer we have chuckled in every chapter about a child's misstating of the Prayer. But *we* easily misunderstand too.

The Lord's Prayer may be committed to memory easily, but it is learned much more slowly by the heart. Shakespeare's *Hamlet* explains the problem, although he probably did not have the Lord's Prayer in mind: "My words fly up, my thoughts remain below: / Words without thoughts never to heaven go."

Following the last petition of the Lord's Prayer comes that incredible doxology: "For thine is the kingdom, and the power, and the glory, for ever. Amen" (Matt. 6:13, KJV). Students of the Bible are surprised to find this doxology left out of most translations of the New Testament.

Early Church Added Doxology

Today archaeology has provided us with Greek manuscripts of the New Testament dating back to the second century. It has been found that none of the early Greek manuscripts have the doxology. In early forms of Christian liturgy, however, the doxology is in the margins in a shortened form: "For Thine is the power and the glory for ever" (Didache). This paralleled the Doxology, or "Gloria," often sung in Jewish Temple worship: "Praise be to his glorious name forever" (Ps. 72:19).

The leader of worship recited the petitions, and the congregation added the doxology of praise from 1 Chron. 29:11.

As the Lord's Prayer was used in early Christian worship, it was very natural for a doxology to be chanted at the conclusion. The leader of worship recited the petitions, and the congregation added the doxology of praise from 1 Chron. 29:11: "Yours, O LORD, is the greatness and the power and the glory and the majesty and the splendor." Wouldn't you have enjoyed hearing the Early Church pray that prayer?

This doxology, originally written in the margins of Christian liturgy, was apparently used so often that it eventually ended up in later Greek manuscripts of the New Testament. Early Christians sang it at the end of the Prayer as a tribute to our "living, reigning, glorified Lord."[1]

Even though these words may not have been in the original prayer given by Jesus, they provide an appropriate and awesome response to the Prayer. These words stand appropriately in our Christian worship because the words are so scripturally based.

God's Greatness Reaffirmed

When this biblical doxology is added, our prayer starts by honoring God and ends by reaffirming His greatness. The model prayer begins with praise to God and ends with praise. Our personal needs fit between as a parenthesis, but at the beginning and end and all the way through we are assured of the incomprehensible adequacy of our Heavenly Father.

"Thine is . . . the glory" directs our thoughts to God the Father, whose glory has shone in the face of Jesus Christ.

Many have suggested that the doxology hints of the doctrine of the Trinity. Henry Alford suggested, for example, "'For Thine is the kingdom' directs our thoughts to God the Son who rules over this kingdom; 'Thine is the power' directs our thoughts to God the Holy Spirit by whose power the Son's kingdom is extended throughout the world; 'Thine is the glory' directs our thoughts to God the Father, whose glory has shone in the face of Jesus Christ."[2] Kingdom, power, and glory are mountain peak ideas.

As we come to the conclusion of the Lord's Prayer, we may want to pray with King Jehoshaphat as he prayed when facing vast enemy armies: "We do not know what to do, but our eyes are upon you" (2 Chron. 20:12). We pray with the little girl who finished her prayer by saying, "Now, dear God, what can I do for You?" The Lord's Prayer draws all kinds of emotions from us.

WE SUBMIT TO GOD'S PURPOSE

The doxology causes us to pray, "For thine is *the kingdom*" (emphasis added). We have already prayed, "Thy kingdom come." Now we pray, "Thine *is* the kingdom" (emphasis added). As we pray, we claim God's kingdom rule in our hearts now. We submit to His Kingship, to the principles of the Kingdom, and to the privileges of the Kingdom even as we pray the Lord's Prayer.

> **Earthly kingdoms keep coming and going, but only of God's kingdom can we say in the continuing present tense, "Thine is *the kingdom*" (emphasis added).**

Early Christians, faced with persecution, came to realize that the real Kingdom did not belong to Rome or to Nero, but to God. Earthly kingdoms keep coming and going, but only of God's kingdom can we say in the continuing present tense, "Thine is *the kingdom*" (emphasis added). God has never abdicated His throne, nor will He abdicate it in the future. We bow in submission to Him. This Kingdom is as up-to-date as tomorrow.

A young husband and father struggled about giving himself and his future to the Lord. A Christian friend said, "I am going to pray for you, and then you can pray for yourself."

As the seeker's turn came to pray, he said, "I don't know how to pray. The only prayer I know is the Lord's Prayer, which I learned when I was a small boy."

"Then pray the Lord's Prayer," the friend said, "but mean every word you say."

Slowly the fellow started praying until he came to the petition: "Thy kingdom come. Thy will be done—*Thy will be done.*"

Grasping his friend's hand, the fellow said, "That's what I want. I want His will done in me." Now the seeker experienced the powerful reality, "For thine is the kingdom." That's something he now knows firsthand. The will of God done in us and the Kingdom having first priority is the Christian's commitment and fulfillment too.

What Message Do We Wear?

A simpleminded, illiterate man in England gave himself to Jesus. He joined the local Salvation Army. His wife didn't know what was taking place, but she knew he was happy. One day he came back from the Salvation Army meeting unhappy.

"What's wrong?" she asked.

"They all have red sweaters," he answered, "and I don't have a red sweater." So she knitted him a red sweater.

The first time he wore his red sweater, he came back from the Salvation Army sad again.

"What's wrong now?" she asked.

"They all have yellow writing on their red sweaters," he answered. The woman, who was illiterate, promised to embroider some yellow writing on his red sweater. She crossed the street to a shop window, copied some letters, and embroidered them on his red sweater.

Off her husband went, wearing his red sweater with yellow writing. He was all smiles when he arrived home from visiting the Salvation Army.

"Did they like your sweater?" she asked.

"Yes."

"Did they like the writing?"

"Yes."

"What did they say?"

"They said they liked the writing on my sweater better than the writing on theirs."

She had unknowingly written across his chest, "This business is under new management."

We celebrate that we are under new management. We can resign as the nervous rulers of our puny universe and rest in the Lord who has given us new life. "For thine is the kingdom."

What are we doing when we honestly, sincerely, intentionally pray the Lord's Prayer?

WE DEPEND ON GOD'S POWER

The doxology says, "For thine is . . . *the power*" (emphasis added).

Devotional writer Mendell Taylor reminds us that "our Father" has "power enough to fling whirling worlds from His fingertips and to keep them moving with clocklike precision in their orbits. He has power to mix the colors of flowers and map the course of atoms. He has power to roll out carpets of green from coast to coast and tack them down with violets and daffodils."[3] F. B. Meyer added, "He has the power to set up His kingdom, to overcome evil with good, hate with love, and darkness with light."[4] God's power works for our good and His glory! And that power is at work in us.

Who's in Charge Here?

Our Father has the power to walk with us day by day, enabling us to be strong and victorious in spite of the worst of circumstances. Paul wrote, "For the kingdom of God is not a matter of talk but of power" (1 Cor. 4:20). "When we pray," G. Ray Jordan wrote, "we link ourselves with the inexhaustible power that spins the universe. Even in asking, our human deficiencies are filled and we arise strengthened and repaired."[5]

Oliver Cromwell, a British political leader, sent a secretary on an important secret mission aboard a ship. Haunted by fear, the secretary thought something would go wrong. The secretary's servant asked, "Master, may I ask you a question?"

"Of course."

"Master, did God rule the world before we were born?"

"Most assuredly He did."

"And will He rule it after we are dead?"

"Certainly," the man answered, quite puzzled.

"Then why can't we let Him rule the present as well?"[6]

The question is for us all—does the almighty God, our Father, control the details of our life? The Bible says, "God is able to make all grace abound to you, so that in all things at all times, having all that you need, you will abound in every good work" (2 Cor. 9:8). What a list—all grace, all things, all times, all you need, every good work! That's power! That's sufficiency!

In 1924 Black opera singer Roland Hayes stood to sing in a concert hall in Berlin. Many in his audience hated American Blacks. Hayes described that night: "At eight o'clock I walked onto the stage . . . a barrage of hisses, full of hatred, greeted me. I felt those hisses as if they were arrows aimed at my breast."

> **With hands folded and eyes closed,**
> **he prayed that God would sweep away**
> **racial hatreds. At last the hisses**
> **died down. Silence.**

That great singer bowed his head and prayed, not that his talents would dazzle the audience, but that God's Spirit would flow through his songs. With hands folded and eyes closed, he prayed that God would sweep away racial hatreds. At last the hisses died down. Silence.

Then Hayes sang the clear notes and message of Schubert's "Thou Art My Peace." When the last tones died away, the crowd responded with deafening applause. Hayes reported about that experience: "It was not a personal victory; it was the victory of God which sang through me. I was allowing myself to be used by a power . . . greater than I."[7] God's power remains available to you for every situation you encounter.

What are we doing when we honestly, sincerely, intentionally pray, "For thine is . . . the power"?

WE SALUTE GOD'S GLORY

The doxology continues, "For thine is . . . *the glory*" (emphasis added).

The excellence of God's character and His marvelous works reflect His glory. A devotional writer gives us a checklist bigger than we can comprehend. He writes, "The term 'glory' is always linked with the blessings God bestows, the beauty He unveils, the benefits He shares, the resources He makes available, and the advantages He provides."[8] The riches of God uncovered in the Lord's Prayer stir us to exalt the name of our Lord.

French soldiers, mortally wounded in battle, would turn toward Napoleon, wave to him, and cry out, "Long live the emperor!" They exalted their emperor with their last breath of loyalty. And someday every knee shall bow and "every tongue confess that Jesus Christ is Lord, to the glory of God the Father" (Phil. 2:11). It is fitting for us to exclaim, "For Thine is . . . the glory." Someone much greater than Napoleon has captured our love and loyalty.

Jesus taught us to pray to "Our Father in heaven." However complicated and incomprehensible is God's greatness, for me the highest glory is His Fatherhood. Nothing my daughters, Shannon and Shelley, can give to me or say about me equals in my heart the times they say with admiration, "He's my father."

Angels serenaded the announcement to shepherds, singing, "Glory to God in the highest" (Luke 2:14).

God gift wrapped Jesus to come among us and to tell us about the Fatherhood of God. Angels serenaded the announcement to shepherds, singing, "Glory to God in the highest" (Luke 2:14). He alone is worthy of our praise.

What are we actually doing when we honestly, sincerely, intentionally pray, "For thine is . . . the glory"?

WE SHARE GOD'S PERSPECTIVE

The doxology says, "For Thine is the kingdom, and the power, and the glory, *for ever*" (emphasis added).

We are not talking here about a one-hour program. We are not talking about short-term commitments between God and those of us who believe and trust Him. It's not like the cynical jeweler's advertisement, "Wedding rings for rent."

When we honestly, sincerely, intentionally pray the Lord's Prayer, we're talking about a relationship with God that lasts *"for ever."* We place our confidence in the ever living Father and in Jesus Christ, who "is the same yesterday, today, and forever" (Heb. 13:8, TEV). That means our God, who looks after us in life, will still be looking out for us for eternity.

Quicken the Pace

Friends asked a Scottish philosopher on his deathbed about his thoughts and hopes. With faltering breath, he exclaimed, "Intense expectations." Me too!

> **Somehow those horses knew that the journey was coming to an end. Sights and scents indicated that home was not far away. They had a spring in their steps.**

The old plow horses worked long days until visibly tired. As evening approached and the farmer headed the team toward home, the horses pricked up their ears and broke into a gentle trot—going faster and faster. Somehow those horses knew that the journey was coming to an end. Sights and scents indicated that home was not far away. They had a spring in their steps.

In the Christian's journey the believer begins at last to sense the lights of home. We experience "intense expectations." The Bible says, "No eye has seen, no ear has heard, no mind has conceived what God has prepared for those who love him" (1 Cor. 2:9).

> **The best is yet to come. Therefore, we begin to see with God's perspective the trials and tests, the separations and setbacks.**

The evening of this old world reminds us that a bright new day dawns tomorrow in God's eternity. And we shall be with our Father forever. The best is yet to come. Therefore, we begin to see with God's perspective the trials and tests, the separations and setbacks. "Thine . . . for ever."

What are we doing when we honestly, sincerely, intentionally pray, "For thine is . . . the glory, for ever"?

WE AFFIRM GOD'S PROMISES

The doxology concludes with one word: "Amen."

When early Christians used this word, it wasn't the empty phrase it is today. People in our day either ignore "Amen" in worship services or throw it around with little meaning. I have noticed some worship leaders now use it as a question: "Amen?" That strips it of all biblical meaning.

An Amen of Trust

Maclaren explained that the "amen" is "the expression of assured expectancy and confidence."[9] "Amen" has Hebrew origins in a verb that signifies, "To be firm, true, faithful, secure." Rather than a request, "So be it," "amen" affirms. "It is true. It is secure and firm."

"Amen" is not a closing punctuation or sign-off. It expresses confident trust that our all-wise Father has heard our prayers and that our all-powerful Father will do what is best for us; therefore we relax in faith.

> **"Amen" says, "I know the answers to these petitions are already on the way."**

Corrie ten Boom exhorted people to nestle rather than to wrestle. Can we nestle in God's promises, or do we fret and struggle over our prayers? A sincere "amen" suggests the same atmosphere of faith expressed by the author of Hebrews: "Now faith is being sure of what we hope for and certain of what we do not see" (Heb. 11:1). In other words, "amen" says, "I know the answers to these petitions are already on the way."

The Lord's Prayer shows us how to pray according to God's will: "This is the confidence we have in approaching God: that if we ask anything according to his will, he hears us. And if we know that he hears us—whatever we ask—we know that we have what we asked of him" (1 John 5:14-15).

Spoken with Authority

We should launch our prayers with expectancy and the certainty of being answered. We must affirm God's promises. The simple word "amen" is significant.

> **Jesus used this expression, "Amen, amen," when He was speaking with God's authority.**

In the four Gospels no one but Jesus utters "amen." More than 24 times Jesus introduces some teaching by saying, "*Amen,*

amen, lego hymin"—"Verily, verily, I say unto you" (KJV). Jesus used this expression, "Amen, amen," when He was speaking with God's authority. It is the New Testament equivalent of the Old Testament phrase "Thus saith the LORD" (KJV). Thus, "amen" is Jesus' seal of authority.

In special high and holy moments, God gave His people permission to make the claim to His authority: "Let all the people say, 'Amen!'" (Ps. 106:48).

Claiming God's Promises

The Lord's Prayer imparts permission to pray and to claim the answers on the authority of God's Word. I love the Bible promise "For no matter how many promises God has made, they are 'Yes' in Christ. And so through him the 'Amen' is spoken by us to the glory of God" (2 Cor. 1:20). Jesus stands behind every "yes" and every "amen" claiming the promises of God.

Luthi explained how the word "amen" was used in the Early Church:

> Thanks to this abundant use of the Amen, the services were rather different from those we know today. The congregation did not sit there silently as if they were not taking part. Any man who was not [teaching or preaching] could at any time join in with his Amen of faith when the Spirit moved him. Through this confirming Amen inspired by the Spirit, a special kind of communion arose between the speaker and those who were listening, and among the listeners themselves.

Today's reformations of worship services could learn from the ancient ways of the affirming "amen" as Luthi suggested:

> The preacher of today is in such a solitary position in his pulpit. Even though he knows that he is accompanied by many a silent Amen, how lonely he is when the community sends him into battle. . . . Things were different in the communities of the New Testament. The Christians in Ephesus, Corinth, or Rome were not giving cheap applause; no, each one of them was taking an active part in the battle of the Spirit and the spirits with his contributory and supporting Amen. What a power of rejoicing when a crowd of believers confirms a prayer of thanks with their "Amen."[10]

In those early days Christians weren't prompted to say "amen" to see if they were still awake. They joined their "amens" to claim the powerful promises of God.

The "amen" is a step of faith so powerful that we begin to act on it. We prayed it. We believe we have been heard. We believe the answer is on the way. Therefore, we act on what we have prayed.

Ben Discovers Father

Ben Hooper never knew his father. That missing security affected him tremendously. He always dreaded the moment when somebody would ask, "Who's your father?" He died a thousand deaths over it. People cruelly began to refer to him as "Ben the bastard boy." His demeanor and outlook bore the terrible lashes of social rejection—an awful ordeal for an innocent child.

Before Ben could respond, the preacher continued, "You, Ben, are a child of God."

One day Ben met a preacher, a man he liked. But eventually the preacher asked that dreaded question, "Ben, who is your father?" Before Ben could respond, the preacher continued, "You, Ben, are a child of God."

That powerful concept changed Ben's life. He was so filled with faith through Jesus Christ that God was His Father that he acted on that faith, and it transformed him. Hooper eventually became governor of Tennessee.

But Hooper's faith discovery works for all who seek the Savior. Who is your Father? You are children of God. "Amen"— we know it's true, and we must act on that truth.

The first time I preached on the last petition, "Deliver us from evil," I received a timely note from a person in our congregation. The second paragraph of the note referred to the illustration of the Indian boy being tested by spending the night alone in the dark woods only to discover in the dawn's early light that his father had been there all the time.

A Father Brings Comfort

The writer of the note commented, "It moved me to tears. I'm just learning that my Heavenly Father was there, even when my drunken father was abusing Mom and all the kids. So sad, but such a comfort now to know I have a 'Father.'" That's the central message of the Lord's Prayer—you have a Father, who is also your God.

I wish that we were all learning to affirm God's promises and His continuing presence—and with a resounding "amen" to the Lord's Prayer—that we would live as children of God.

I once heard Haddon Robinson preach in Moody Memorial Church in Chicago. He said that when his children were small, he would play a game with them by putting several coins in his hand.

So they'd sit in my lap, and they'd pry my hand open.

"The rules of the game were that once they got the finger open, I would leave it open," he said. "So they'd sit in my lap, and they'd pry my hand open. Then finally they'd get the pennies that were there. When they got the pennies, they would jump down from my lap with a kind of glee and push my hand away.

The purpose of prayer is not to get God's pennies; it's to get hold of God.

"Just kids, just children. Yet how many times when we come to pray, what we're concerned about are the pennies in God's hand. We need a new job, Lord. We're sick and we need health. Lord, I need a good grade on that exam. We pray and pry loose God's fingers and take the pennies, and we push His hand away. The purpose of prayer is not to get God's pennies; it's to get hold of God."[11]

There you have it: Our Heavenly Father is the Object of our quest. "Lord, teach us to pray" (Luke 11:1).

Chapter 10

Insights to Transform Your Praying

- The Lord's Prayer assures us of God's adequacy.

- "Thine is the glory" directs our prayer thoughts to the majesty and holiness of God.

- Other kingdoms rise and fall, but the kingdom of God lasts forever.

- God's power is available for every situation you encounter.

- God gift wrapped Jesus to show us what the Father is really like.

- The Lord's Prayer reminds us that the best is yet to come.

- "Amen" expresses confident trust that our all-wise Father has heard our prayer and is already answering it.

- The central message of the Lord's Prayer is that you have a Father who is also your God.

Appendix A

A Responsive Reading on the Lord's Prayer

PASTOR: I cannot say, *"Our"*
PEOPLE: If my religion has no room for other people and their needs.

PASTOR: I cannot say, *"Father"*
PEOPLE: If I do not demonstrate this relationship in my daily life.

PASTOR: I cannot say, *"which art in heaven"*
PEOPLE: If all my interests and pursuits are earthly things.

PASTOR: I cannot say, *"Hallowed be thy name"*
PEOPLE: If I, who am called by His name, am not holy.

PASTOR: I cannot say, *"Thy kingdom come"*
PEOPLE: If I am unwilling to give up sovereignty and accept the reign of God.

PASTOR: I cannot say, *"Thy will be done"*
PEOPLE: If I am unwilling or resentful of having Him in my life.

PASTOR: I cannot say, *"In earth, as it is in heaven"*
PEOPLE: Unless I am truly ready to give myself to His service here and now.

PASTOR: I cannot say, *"Give us this daily bread"*
PEOPLE: Without expending honest effort for it, or by ignoring the needs of my fellowmen.

PASTOR: I cannot say, *"Forgive us our debts, as we forgive our debtors"*
PEOPLE: If I continue to harbor a grudge against anyone.

PASTOR: I cannot say, *"Lead us not into temptation"*
PEOPLE: If I deliberately choose to remain in a situation where I am likely to be tempted.

PASTOR: I cannot say, *"Deliver us from evil"*

PEOPLE: If I am not prepared to fight in the spiritual realm with the weapon of prayer.

PASTOR: I cannot say, *"Thine is the kingdom, and the power, and the glory"*

PEOPLE: If I do not give disciplined obedience; if I fear what neighbors and friends may say or do; if I seek my own glory first.

PASTOR: I cannot say, *"Amen"*

PEOPLE: Unless I can honestly say also, "Cost what it may, this is my prayer."

Appendix B

THE LORD'S PRAYER

submitted by Jeanette Larrew

This is how you shouLd pray: "Our Father
in heaven, hallOwed be your name:
youR
kingDom

Come, your will
be done on eartH
As it is in
heaveN. Give us today our
daily bread. ForGive us our debts,
as wE also have forgiven our debtors.

Lead us not into teMptation, but deliver
us from Evil.

For yours is the kingdom
and the power
and the glory
forever.
Amen.

Notes

Preface

1. Will Durant, *Our Oriental Heritage: The Story of Civilization*, Part I (New York: Simon & Schuster, 1954).

Chapter 1

1. John MacArthur Jr., *Jesus' Pattern of Prayer* (Chicago: Moody Press, 1981), 15.

2. W. E. McCumber, *A Little Book About Prayer* (Kansas City: Beacon Hill Press of Kansas City, 1980), 29.

3. William H. Erb, *The Lord's Prayer* (Reading, Pa.: I. M. Beaver, Publisher, 1908), 28.

4. E. Stanley Jones, *The Way* (Garden City, N.Y.: Doubleday and Co., a Doubleday Galilee Book, 1978), 216.

5. MacArthur, *Jesus' Pattern of Prayer*, 19.

6. William Barclay, *The Gospel of Matthew*, vol. 1, in The Daily Study Bible Series (Philadelphia: Westminster Press, 1958), 199.

7. Ibid.

8. Erb, *Lord's Prayer*, 27.

9. Aaron N. Meckel, *Faith Alive!* (Grand Rapids: Zondervan Publishing House, 1965), 17.

10. Certain illustrations and quotations have become a part of notes for preaching and teaching that I have developed over a number of years. Although I am certain of the accuracy of these materials, I do not have the original sources. Several other times in this book I will use other such quotations and illustrations. I will not footnote them. If sources are located, they will be included in reprints of this book.

11. F. B. Meyer, *The Sermon on the Mount* (Grand Rapids: Baker Book House, 1959), 111.

12. John Sutherland Bonnell, *The Practice and Power of Prayer* (Philadelphia: Westminster Press, 1954), 61.

13. *Daily Guideposts: 1982* (Carmel, N.Y.: Guideposts Associates, 1981), 304.

14. William Folprecht, source unknown.

Chapter 2

1. H. S. Vigeveno, *Jesus, the Revolutionary* (Glendale, Calif.: G/L Publications, G/L Regal Books, 1967), 100.

2. MacArthur, *Jesus' Pattern of Prayer*, 31.

3. Helmut Thielicke, *Our Heavenly Father*, trans. John W. Doberstein (New York: Harper and Row, Publishers, 1960), 21.

4. Maxie D. Dunnam, *Exodus*, OT vol. 2 of *The Communicator's Commentary*, ed. Lloyd J. Ogilvie (Waco, Tex.: Word, 1987), 346.

5. Harry Rimmer, *The Prayer Perfect* (New York: Fleming H. Revell Co., 1940), 21.

6. Ibid.

7. Archibald M. Hunter, *A Pattern for Life* (Philadelphia: Westminster Press, 1953), 67.

8. Mendell Taylor, *Devotional Dimensions in the Lord's Prayer* (Kansas City: Beacon Hill Press of Kansas City, 1975), 11.

9. Barclay, *Gospel of Matthew*, 1:202-3.

10. Robert R. Kopp, *Praying like Jesus: Sermons on the Lord's Prayer* (Kansas City: Pedestal Press, 1986), 17.

11. James D. Hamilton, *The Faces of God* (Kansas City: Beacon Hill Press of Kansas City, 1984), 81.

12. Charlie Shedd, *Promises to Peter: Building a Bridge from Parent to Child* (Waco, Tex.: Word Books Publisher, 1970), 70.

13. W. Phillip Keller, *A Layman Looks at the Lord's Prayer* (Chicago: Moody Press, 1976), 26.

14. Clyde E. Fant Jr. and William M. Pinson Jr., eds., *Twenty Centuries of Great Preaching* (Waco, Tex.: Word Books, Publisher, 1971), 11:102.

15. C. S. Cowles, "Lesson 12: Sorrow over the Demise of a Nation," *Adult Teacher* (Kansas City: Nazarene Publishing House, Feb. 16, 1986), 80-81.

16. Notes the author took on a message by Lyle Pointer.

17. Meckel, *Faith Alive!* 118.

18. G. Ray Jordan, *Prayer That Prevails* (New York: Macmillan Co., 1958), 144.

19. John T. Seamands, *Tell It Well: Communicating the Gospel Across Cultures* (Kansas City: Beacon Hill Press of Kansas City, 1981), 84-85.

20. Charles L. Allen, *In Quest of God's Power* (Old Tappan, N.J.: Fleming H. Revell Co., 1952), 51.

Chapter 3

1. Taylor, *Devotional Dimensions*, 12.

2. Ralph Earle, *Word Meanings in the New Testament* (Kansas City: Beacon Hill Press of Kansas City, 1980), 1:28.

3. Keller, *Layman Looks*, 49.

4. Hunter, *Pattern for Life*, 66.

5. Edward W. H. Vick, *Our Lord's Prayer: A Devotional Study* (Mountain View, Calif.: Pacific Press Publishing Association, 1977), 17.

6. Keller, *Layman Looks*, 48.

7. Erb, *Lord's Prayer*, 69.

8. Leslie B. Flynn, *Worship: Together We Celebrate* (Wheaton, Ill.: SP Publications, Victor Books, 1983), 19.

9. MacArthur, *Jesus' Pattern of Prayer*, 49.

10. William E. Yeager, *Who's Holding the Umbrella?* (Nashville: Thomas Nelson Publishers, 1984), 182.

11. Barclay, *Gospel of Matthew*, 1:206.

12. Rimmer, *Prayer Perfect*, 35.

13. Barclay, *Gospel of Matthew*, 1:208.

14. Dunnam, *Exodus*, 61.

15. Willie B. Raborn, "A New Pair of Shoes," *Guideposts*, April 1976, 24-26.

Chapter 4

1. William Barclay, *Fishers of Men* (Philadelphia: Westminster Press, 1966), 68.

2. Hunter, *Pattern for Life*, 68-69.

3. Barclay, *Gospel of Matthew*, 1:211-12.

4. E. Stanley Jones, *Growing Spiritually* (New York: Abingdon Press, 1953), 281.

5. Rimmer, *Prayer Perfect*, 56.

6. Source unknown.

7. Rimmer, *Prayer Perfect*, 57-58.

8. Dwight L. Carlson, *Living God's Will* (Old Tappan, N.J.: Fleming H. Revell Co., 1976), 78.

9. MacArthur, *Jesus' Pattern of Prayer*, 67.

10. Kopp, *Praying like Jesus*, 29.

11. E. Stanley Jones, *The Word Became Flesh* (New York: Abingdon Press, 1963), 209.

12. Kopp, *Praying like Jesus*, 29.

13. Barclay, *Gospel of Matthew*, 1:212.

14. Erb, *Lord's Prayer*, 114.

Chapter 5

1. Charles L. Allen, *God's Psychiatry* (New York: Fleming H. Revell Co., 1953), 106.
2. Ralph Cushman, *I Have a Stewardship: A Book of Worship* (New York: Abingdon Press, 1939), 43.
3. T. W. Willingham, *A Second Basket of Crumbs* (Kansas City: Beacon Hill Press of Kansas City, 1975), 22.
4. Erb, *Lord's Prayer*, 132-33.
5. Dunnam, *Exodus*, 168.
6. Keller, *Layman Looks*, 65-66.
7. Taylor, *Devotional Dimensions*, 25-26.
8. Dunnam, *Exodus*, 169.
9. E. Stanley Jones, *Victorious Living* (New York: Abingdon-Cokesbury Press, 1936), 137.
10. Dunnam, *Exodus*, 105.
11. Source unknown.
12. Keller, *Layman Looks*, 89-95.

Chapter 6

1. MacArthur, *Jesus' Pattern of Prayer*, 88.
2. Barclay, *Gospel of Matthew*, 1:217-18.
3. Rimmer, *Prayer Perfect*, 78.
4. Tim Hansel, *When I Relax I Feel Guilty* (Elgin, Ill.: David C. Cook Publishing Co., 1979), 77.
5. Source unknown.
6. MacArthur, *Jesus' Pattern of Prayer*, 88.
7. J. B. Chapman, *Singing in the Shadows* (Kansas City: Nazarene Publishing House, Kingshiway Press, 1941), 87.
8. Thomas A. Carruth, *Total Prayer for Total Living* (Grand Rapids: Zondervan Publishing House, 1962), 27.
9. Hansel, *When I Relax I Feel Guilty*, 70.
10. Howard Butt, *The Velvet Covered Brick: Christian Leadership in an Age of Rebellion* (New York: Harper and Row, Publishers, 1973), 122.
11. Mrs. Bud Robinson, *Buddie and I* (1913; reprint, Kansas City: Nazarene Publishing House, 1987), 39-40.
12. R. T. Williams, *Attitudes and Relationships* (PALCON reprint, Kansas City: Beacon Hill Press of Kansas City, 1976), 116.
13. Ibid.
14. Erb, *Lord's Prayer*, 155.
15. Barclay, *Gospel of Matthew*, 1:219.
16. Rimmer, *Prayer Perfect*, 91-93.
17. Reuben Welch, *Luke*, vol. 3 of *Beacon Bible Expositions* (Kansas City: Beacon Hill Press of Kansas City, 1974), 112.
18. Barclay, *Gospel of Matthew*, 1:220.
19. Howard A. Snyder, *The Community of the King* (Downers Grove, Ill.: InterVarsity Press, 1978), 190-91.
20. C. William Fisher, *When You Pray, Say . . . Give Us This Day Our Daily Bread* (Kansas City: *Showers of Blessing*, Nazarene Radio League, n.d.).

Chapter 7

1. Ruth Bell in an unidentified clipping from *Reader's Digest*.
2. Earle, *Word Meanings*, 1:29.
3. Source unknown.
4. MacArthur, *Jesus' Pattern of Prayer*, 106.
5. Lloyd J. Ogilvie, *Congratulations, God Believes in You!* (Waco, Tex.: Word Books,

1980), 43.

6. Marc Boegner, *The Prayer of the Church Universal,* trans. Howard Schomer (New York: Abingdon Press, 1954), 105.

7. W. T. Purkiser, *These Earthen Vessels* (Kansas City: Beacon Hill Press of Kansas City, 1985), 85.

8. Jordan, *Prayer That Prevails,* 109.

9. James S. Stewart, *A Faith to Proclaim* (New York: Charles Scribner's Sons, 1953), 50.

10. Thielicke, *Our Heavenly Father,* 91.

11. Ibid.

12. Daniel D. Walker, *The Human Problems of the Minister* (New York: Harper and Brothers, 1960), 5.

13. Paul H. Hetrick, "No 'Pay Back' at the Cross," *Herald of Holiness,* April 15, 1976, 4-5.

14. Kopp, *Praying like Jesus,* 50.

15. MacArthur, *Jesus' Pattern of Prayer,* 112.

16. Seamands, *Tell It Well,* 80.

17. Charles L. Allen, *Prayer Changes Things* (Westwood, N.J.: Fleming H. Revell Co., 1965), 26.

18. Ibid.

19. Bruce Larson, *Luke,* NT vol. 3 of *The Communicator's Commentary,* ed. Lloyd J. Ogilvie (Waco, Tex.: Word Books, Publisher, 1983), 192-93.

Chapter 8

1. Kopp, *Praying like Jesus,* 51.

2. Clifton J. Allen, ed., *The Broadman Bible Commentary* (Nashville: Broadman Press, 1969), 8:116.

3. William Barclay, *The Old Law and the New Law* (Philadelphia: Westminster Press, 1972), 82.

4. Taylor, *Devotional Dimensions,* 46.

5. Allen, *God's Psychiatry,* 116.

6. W. E. Sangster and Leslie Davison, *The Pattern of Prayer* (London: Epworth Press, 1962), 72.

7. Jordan, *Prayer That Prevails,* 104-5.

8. *Daily Guideposts: 1982,* 87.

9. Paul Martin, *Have a Good Day* (Kansas City: Beacon Hill Press of Kansas City, 1971), 20.

10. Keller, *Layman Looks,* 123.

11. Kopp, *Praying like Jesus,* 54.

Chapter 9

1. William Barclay, *Marching Orders,* ed. Denis Duncan (Philadelphia: Westminster Press, 1973), 140.

2. Adam Clarke, *Clarke's Commentary* (New York: Abingdon Press, n.d.), 5:87.

3. Barclay, *Gospel of Matthew,* 226.

4. Ibid., 230.

5. Ibid., 232.

6. Walter Luthi, *The Lord's Prayer,* trans. Kurt Schoenenberger (Richmond, Va.: John Knox Press, 1962), 59.

7. Kopp, *Praying like Jesus,* 67.

8. Barclay, *Gospel of Matthew,* 226.

9. Allen, *God's Psychiatry,* 120.

10. Kopp, *Praying like Jesus,* 61.

11. Welch, *Luke,* 120.

12. Jones, *The Way,* 223.

13. Allen, *God's Psychiatry*, 125.

14. Clovis G. Chappell, *Sermons on the Lord's Prayer and Other Prayers of Jesus* (New York: Abingdon Press, 1934), 135.

15. Larson, *Luke*, 193.

16. Boegner, *Prayer of the Church Universal*, 107.

17. *Daily Guideposts: 1982*, 77.

Chapter 10

1. Meckel, *Faith Alive!* 124.

2. James G. S. S. Thomson, *The Praying Christ: A Study of Jesus' Doctrine and Practice of Prayer* (Grand Rapids: Wm. B. Eerdmans Publishing Co., 1959), 100.

3. Taylor, *Devotional Dimensions*, 66.

4. Meyer, *Sermon on the Mount*, 131.

5. Jordan, *Prayer That Prevails*, 142-43.

6. Ibid., 145.

7. Ibid., 142.

8. Taylor, *Devotional Dimensions*, 67.

9. Alexander Maclaren, *Expositions of Holy Scripture* (Grand Rapids: Wm. B. Eerdmans Publishing Co., 1944), 6:295.

10. Luthi, *Lord's Prayer*, 102-3.

11. Haddon Robinson, "Prayer in the Life of Jesus," in *Moody Founder's Week Conference Messages*, February 1-7, 1988 (Chicago: Moody Bible Institute, 1988), 233-34.

Bibliography

Alford, Henry. *The New Testament for English Readers*. Chicago: Moody Press, n.d.

Allen, Charles L. *God's Psychiatry*. New York: Fleming H. Revell Co., 1953.

————. *In Quest of God's Power*. Old Tappan, N.J.: Fleming H. Revell Co., 1952.

————. *Prayer Changes Things*. Westwood, N.J.: Fleming H. Revell Co., 1965.

Allen, Clifton J., ed. *The Broadman Bible Commentary*. Vol. 8. Nashville: Broadman Press, 1969.

Barclay, William. *Fishers of Men*. Philadelphia: Westminster Press, 1966.

————. *The Gospel of Matthew*, vol. 1. The Daily Study Bible Series. Philadelphia: Westminster Press, 1958.

————. *Marching Orders*. Ed. Denis Duncan. Philadelphia: Westminster Press, 1973.

————. *The Old Law and the New Law*. Philadelphia: Westminster Press, 1972.

Boegner, Marc. *The Prayer of the Church Universal*. Trans. Howard Schomer. New York: Abingdon Press, 1954.

Bonnell, John Sutherland. *The Practice and Power of Prayer*. Philadelphia: Westminster Press, 1954.

Briscoe, Stuart. *How to Be a Motivated Christian*. Wheaton, Ill.: SP Publications, Victor Books, 1987.

Butt, Howard. *The Velvet Covered Brick: Christian Leadership in an Age of Rebellion*. New York: Harper and Row, Publishers, 1973.

Carlson, Dwight L. *Living God's Will*. Old Tappan, N.J.: Fleming H. Revell Co., 1976.

Carruth, Thomas A. *Total Prayer for Total Living*. Grand Rapids: Zondervan Publishing House, 1962.

Chapman, J. B. *Singing in the Shadows*. Kansas City: Nazarene Publishing House, Kingshiway Press, 1941.

Chappell, Clovis G. *Sermons on the Lord's Prayer and Other Prayers of Jesus*. New York: Abingdon Press, 1934.

Clarke, Adam. *Clarke's Commentary*. Vol. 5. New York: Abingdon Press, n.d.

Cushman, Ralph. *I Have a Stewardship*. New York: Abingdon Press, 1939.

Daily Guideposts: 1982. Carmel, N.Y.: Guideposts Associates, 1981.

Dunnam, Maxie D. *Exodus*. OT vol. 2, *The Communicator's Commentary*, ed. Lloyd J. Ogilvie. Waco, Tex.: Word, 1987.

Earle, Ralph. *Word Meanings in the New Testament*. Vol. 1. Kansas City: Beacon Hill Press of Kansas City, 1980.

Erb, William H. *The Lord's Prayer*. Reading, Pa.: I. M. Beaver, Publisher, 1908.

Evans, Louis H. *Youth Seeks a Master*. Westwood, N.J.: Fleming H. Revell Co., 1954.

Fant, Clyde E., Jr., and William M. Pinson Jr., eds. *Twenty Centuries of Great Preaching*. Vol. 11. Waco, Tex.: Word Books, Publisher, 1971.

Fisher, C. William. *When You Pray, Say . . . Give Us This Day Our Daily Bread*. Kansas City: *Showers of Blessing*, Nazarene Radio League, n.d.

Flynn, Leslie B. *Worship: Together We Celebrate*. Wheaton, Ill.: SP Publications, Victor Books, 1983.

Graham, Billy. *A Vision Imparted*.

Hamilton, James D. *The Faces of God*. Kansas City: Beacon Hill Press of Kansas City, 1984.

Hansel, Tim. *When I Relax I Feel Guilty*. Elgin, Ill.: David C. Cook Publishing Co., 1979.

Hetrick, Paul H. "No 'Pay Back' at the Cross." *Herald of Holiness*, April 15, 1976.

Hunter, Archibald M. *A Pattern for Life*. Philadelphia: Westminster Press, 1953.

Jones, E. Stanley. *Growing Spiritually*. New York: Abingdon Press, 1953.

———. *Victorious Living*. New York: Abingdon-Cokesbury Press, 1936.

————. *The Way*. Garden City, N.Y.: Doubleday and Co., a Doubleday Galilee Book, 1978.

————. *The Word Became Flesh.* New York: Abingdon Press, 1963.

Jordan, G. Ray. *Prayer That Prevails.* New York: Macmillan Co., 1958.

Keller, W. Phillip. *A Layman Looks at the Lord's Prayer.* Chicago: Moody Press, 1976.

Kopp, Robert R. *Praying like Jesus: Sermons on the Lord's Prayer.* Kansas City: Pedestal Press, 1986.

Larson, Bruce. *Luke.* NT vol. 3 of *The Communicator's Commentary,* ed. Lloyd J. Ogilvie. Waco, Tex.: Word Books, Publisher, 1983.

Luthi, Walter. *The Lord's Prayer.* Trans. Kurt Schoenenberger. Richmond, Va.: John Knox Press, 1962.

MacArthur, John, Jr. *Jesus' Pattern of Prayer.* Chicago: Moody Press, 1981.

Maclaren, Alexander. *Expositions of Holy Scripture.* Vol. 6. Grand Rapids: Wm. B. Eerdmans Publishing Co., 1944.

Martin, Paul. *Have a Good Day.* Kansas City: Beacon Hill Press of Kansas City, 1971.

McCumber, W. E. *A Little Book About Prayer.* Kansas City: Beacon Hill Press of Kansas City, 1980.

Meckel, Aaron N. *Faith Alive!* Grand Rapids: Zondervan Publishing House, 1965.

Meyer, F. B. *The Sermon on the Mount.* Grand Rapids: Baker Book House, 1959.

Ogilvie, Lloyd J. *Congratulations, God Believes in You!* Waco, Tex.: Word Books, 1980.

Purkiser, W. T. *These Earthen Vessels.* Kansas City: Beacon Hill Press of Kansas City, 1985.

Raborn, Willie B. "A New Pair of Shoes." *Guideposts,* April 1976.

Rice, M. S. *The Expected Church.* New York: Abingdon Press, 1923.

Rimmer, Harry. *The Prayer Perfect.* New York: Fleming H. Revell Co., 1940.

Robinson, Haddon. "Prayer in the Life of Jesus." In *Moody Founder's Week Conference Messages,* February 1-7, 1988. Chicago: Moody Bible Institute, 1988.

Robinson, Mrs. Bud. *Buddie and I.* 1913. Reprint, Kansas City: Nazarene Publishing House, 1987.

Sangster, W. E., and Leslie Davison. *The Pattern of Prayer.* London: Epworth Press, 1962

Schuller, Robert H. *You Are Wonderful.* Norwalk, Conn.: C. R. Gibson Co., 1987.

Seamands, John T. *Tell It Well: Communicating the Gospel Across Cultures.* Kansas City: Beacon Hill Press of Kansas City, 1981.

Snyder, Howard A. *The Community of the King.* Downers Grove, Ill.: InterVarsity Press, 1978.

Stewart, James S. *A Faith to Proclaim.* New York: Charles Scribner's Sons, 1953.

Taylor, Mendell. *Devotional Dimensions in the Lord's Prayer.* Kansas City: Beacon Hill Press of Kansas City, 1975.

Thielicke, Helmut. *Our Heavenly Father.* Trans. John W. Doberstein. New York: Harper and Row, Publishers, 1960.

Thomson, James G. S. S. *The Praying Christ: A Study of Jesus' Doctrine and Practice of Prayer.* Grand Rapids: Wm. B. Eerdmans Publishing Co., 1959.

Vick, Edward W. H. *Our Lord's Prayer: A Devotional Study.* Mountain View, Calif.: Pacific Press Publishing Association, 1977.

Vigeveno, H. S. *Jesus, the Revolutionary.* Glendale, Calif.: G/L Publications, G/L Regal Books, 1967.

Walker, Daniel D. *The Human Problems of the Minister.* New York: Harper and Brothers, 1960.

Walker, Herb. *The Happy Clergy.* Amarillo, Tex.: Baxter Lane Co., 1977.

Welch, Reuben. *Luke.* Vol. 3, *Beacon Bible Expositions.* Kansas City: Beacon Hill Press of Kansas City, 1974.

Williams, R. T. *Attitudes and Relationships.* PALCON reprint, Kansas City: Beacon Hill Press of Kansas City, 1976.

Willingham, T. W. *A Second Basket of Crumbs.* Kansas City: Beacon Hill Press of Kansas City, 1975.

Yeager, William E. *Who's Holding the Umbrella?* Nashville: Thomas Nelson Publishers, 1984.